EVERYMAN,
I WILL GO WITH THEE
AND BE THY GUIDE,
IN THY MOST NEED
TO GO BY THY SIDE

EVERYMAN'S LIBRARY
POCKET POETS

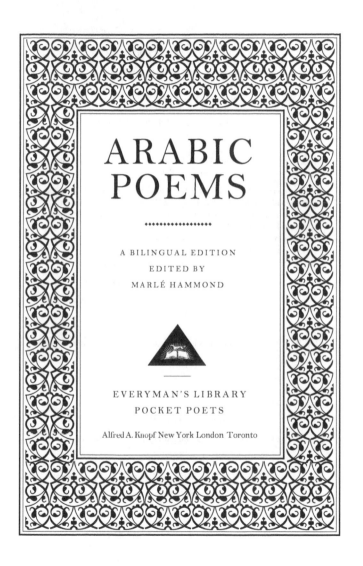

ARABIC
POEMS

••••••••••••••••••••

A BILINGUAL EDITION

EDITED BY

MARLÉ HAMMOND

EVERYMAN'S LIBRARY
POCKET POETS

Alfred A. Knopf New York London Toronto

THIS IS A BORZOI BOOK
PUBLISHED BY ALFRED A. KNOPF

This selection by Marlé Hammond first published in
Everyman's Library, 2014
Copyright © 2014 by Everyman's Library

Tenth printing (US)

A list of acknowledgments to copyright owners appears at the back
of this volume.

All rights reserved. Published in the United States by Alfred A. Knopf,
a division of Penguin Random House LLC, New York, and in Canada by
Penguin Random House Canada Limited, Toronto. Distributed by Penguin
Random House LLC, New York. Published in the United Kingdom by
Everyman's Library, 50 Albemarle Street, London W1S 4BD and
distributed by Penguin Random House UK,
20 Vauxhall Bridge Road, London SW1V 2SA.

www.randomhouse.com/everymans
www.everymanslibrary.co.uk

ISBN 978-0-375-71243-2 (US)
978-1-84159-798-0 (UK)

A CIP catalogue record for this book is available from the British Library

Typography by Peter B. Willberg

Typeset in the UK by AccComputing, Wincanton, Somerset

Arabic typesetting by Feri Jokar

Printed and bound in Germany by GGP Media GmbH, Pössneck

CONTENTS

FOREWORD

Arabic poetry is as vast as it is deep, encompassing all manner of poetic expression from Morocco to Iraq and spanning more than fifteen centuries. In its early stages it formed part of an oral tradition, and there were systematic and collective efforts to transmit it to later generations. Poetry not only entertained and delighted, it also served to memorialize individuals, communities and events. When scholars and scribes of the second and third Islamic centuries (ninth and tenth centuries, CE) began to record this inheritance in writing, it served as an important foundation for knowledge. Even today, it has pride of place in the public domain, engaging the elites and the masses in equal measure, albeit in different registers.

This anthology attempts to capture the breadth and depth of the Arabic poetic legacy through its inclusion of pieces composed from pre-Islamic times through to the twenty-first century. It does not claim to offer a representative sampling, however. Instead, in an effort to lend coherence to the anthology and to appeal to the lay reader, I have selected poems reflecting sentiments of desire or longing, poems whose most immediate meanings transcend the limitations of time and space. Such expressions of yearning occur in a wide variety of genres. In addition to straightforward love poetry, or *ghazal*, we find mystical poems and elegies. The nostalgic stance of the heroic odes, including the celebrated *Mu'allaqat*, with their contemplation of the beloved's abandoned campsite and their emphasis on cycles of death and rebirth, famine and feasting, leave the poetic persona and reader alike aching for the spring rains. Al-Shanfara's 'L-Poem', ostensibly a poem of rejection which subverts tribal values, strikes one as a portrait of a terribly lonely person longing for companionship and family. The ancient genre of 'longing for homelands' (*al-hanin ila al-awtan*), represented here by the 'Song of Maisuna', finds echoes in the selections of the exiled modern poets. Some of the pieces in the anthology read as expressions of sheer delight, or as an appreciation of everyday affairs, while others, particularly among the modern selections, express an anti-nostalgic and deeply felt yearning for change. It is hoped that the reader will find these poems diverting, moving and provocative.

Marlé Hammond

Note:
Pre-modern Arabic poems were not given titles. The titles for these selections have either been assigned by the translators or drawn from the wording of the poem (usually the opening verse).

ARABIC
POEMS

قِفَا نَبْكِ مِنْ ذِكْرى حَبِيبٍ وَمَنْزِلِ
بِسِقْطِ اللَّوى بَيْنَ الدَّخُولِ فَحَوْمَلِ

فَتُوضِحَ فالْمِقْرَاةِ لَمْ يَعْفُ رَسْمُهَا
لِمَا نَسَجَتْهَا مِنْ جَنُوبٍ وَشَمْأَلِ

تَرى بَعَرَ الأَرْآمِ فِي عَرَصَاتِهَا
وَقِيعَانِهَا كَأَنَّهُ حَبُّ فُلْفُلِ

كَأَنِّي غَدَاةَ الْبَيْنِ يَوْمَ تَحَمَّلُوا
لَدَى سَمُرَاتِ الْحَيِّ نَاقِفُ حَنْظَلِ

وُقُوفاً بِهَا صَحْبِي عَلَيَّ مَطِيَّهُمْ
يَقُولُونَ لَا تَهْلِكْ أَسًى وَتَجَمَّلِ

وَإِنَّ شِفَائِي عَبْرَةٌ مُهَرَاقَةٌ
فَهَلْ عِنْدَ رَسْمٍ دَارِسٍ مِنْ مُعَوَّلِ

كَدَأْبِكَ مِنْ أُمِّ الْحُوَيْرِثِ قَبْلَهَا
وَجَارَتِهَا أُمِّ الرَّبَابِ بِمَأْسَلِ

إِذَا قَامَتَا تَضَوَّعَ الْمِسْكُ مِنْهُما
نَسِيمَ الصَّبَا جَاءَتْ بِرَيَّا الْقَرَنْفُلِ

فَفَاضَتْ دُمُوعُ الْعَيْنِ مِنِّي صَبَابَةً
عَلَى النَّحْرِ حَتَّى بَلَّ دَمْعِيَ مِحْمَلِي

أَلَا رُبَّ يَوْمٍ لَكَ مِنْهُنَّ صَالِح
وَلَا سِيَّمَا يَوْمٌ بِدَارَةِ جُلْجُلِ

MU'ALLAQA

Weep, ah weep love's losing, love's with its dwelling-place
    set where the hills divide Dakhúli and Háumali.

Túdiha and Mikrat! There the hearth-stones of her stand
    where the South and North winds cross-weave the
    sand-furrows.

See the white-doe droppings strewn by the wind on them,
    black on her floors forsaken, fine-grain of peppercorns.

Here it was I watched her, lading her load-camels, stood by
    these thorn-trees weeping tears as of colocynth.

Here my twin-friends waited, called to me camel-borne:
    Man! not of grief thou diest. Take thy pain patiently.

Not though tears assuage thee, deem it beseemeth thee thus
    for mute stones to wail thee, all thy foes witnesses.

What though fortune flout thee! Thus Om Howéyrith did,
    thus did thy Om Rebábi, fooled thee in Másali.

O, where these two tented, sweet was the breath of them,
    sweet as of musk their fragrance, sweet as garánfoli.

Mourned I for them long days, wept for the love of them,
    tears on my bosom raining, tears on my sword-handle.

Yet, was I un-vanquished. Had I not happiness, I, at their
    hands in Dáret, Dáret of Júljuli?

وَيَوْمَ عَقَرْتُ لِلْعَذَارَى مَطِيَّتِي
فَيَا عَجَبًا مِنْ كُورِهَا الْمُتَحَمِّلِ

فَظَلَّ الْعَذَارَى يَرْتَمِينَ بِلَحْمِهَا
وَشَحْمٍ كَهُدَّابِ الدِّمَقْسِ الْمُفَتَّلِ

وَيَوْمَ دَخَلْتُ الْخِدْرَ خِدْرَ عُنَيْزَةٍ
فَقَالَتْ لَكَ الْوَيْلَاتُ إِنَّكَ مُرْجِلِي

تَقُولُ وَقَدْ مَالَ الْغَبِيطُ بِنَا مَعًا
عَقَرْتَ بَعِيرِي يَا امْرَأَ الْقَيْسِ فَانْزِلِ

فَقُلْتُ لَهَا سِيرِي وَأَرْخِي زِمَامَهُ
وَلَا تُبْعِدِينِي مِنْ جَنَاكِ الْمُعَلَّلِ

فَمِثْلِكِ حُبْلَى قَدْ طَرَقْتُ وَمُرْضِعٍ
فَأَلْهَيْتُهَا عَنْ ذِي تَمَائِمَ مُحْوِلِ

إِذَا مَا بَكَى مِنْ خَلْفِهَا انْصَرَفَتْ لَهُ
بِشِقٍّ وَتَحْتِي شِقُّهَا لَمْ يُحَوَّلِ

وَيَوْمًا عَلَى ظَهْرِ الْكَثِيبِ تَعَذَّرَتْ
عَلَيَّ وَآلَتْ حَلْفَةً لَمْ تَحَلَّلِ

أَفَاطِمَ مَهْلًا بَعْضَ هذَا التَّدَلُّلِ
وَإِنْ كُنْتِ قَدْ أَزْمَعْتِ صَرْمِي فَأَجْمِلِي

أَغَرَّكِ مِنِّي أَنَّ حُبَّكِ قَاتِلِي
وَأَنَّكِ مَهْمَا تَأْمُرِي الْقَلْبَ يَفْعَلِ

وَإِنْ تَكُ قَدْ سَاءَتْكِ مِنِّي خَلِيقَةٌ
فَسُلِّي ثِيَابِي مِنْ ثِيَابِكِ تَنْسُلِ

O that day of all days! Slew I my milch-camel, feasted the
    maidens gaily, – well did they load for me!
Piled they high the meat-strings. All day they pelted me,
    pelted themselves with fatness, fringes of camel-meat.
Climbed I to her howdah, sat with Onéyzata, while at my
    raid she chided: Man! Must I walk afoot?
Swayed the howdah wildly, she and I close in it: there!
    my beast's back is galled now. Slave of Grief, down
    with thee.
Answered I: Nay, sweet heart, loosen the rein of him. Think
    not to stay my kisses. Here will I harvest them.
Wooed have I thy equals, maidens and wedded ones.
    Her, the nursling's mother, did I not win to her?
What though he wailed loudly, babe of the amulets, turned
    she not half towards him, half of her clasped to me?
Woe is me, the hard heart! How did she mock at me, high on
    the sand-hill sitting, vowing to leave and go!
Fátma, nay, my own love, though thou wouldst break with
    me, still be thou kind awhile now, leave me not utterly.
Clean art thou mistaken. Love is my malady. Ask me the
    thing thou choosest. Straight will I execute.
If so be thou findest ought in thy lover wrong, cast from thy
    back my garments, moult thee my finery.
Woe is me, the hard heart! When did tears trouble thee save
    for my soul's worse wounding, stricken and near to die?

وَمَا ذَرَفَتْ عَيْنَاكِ إِلَّا لِتَضْرِبِي

بِسَهْمَيْكِ فِي أَعْشَارِ قَلْبٍ مُقَتَّلِ

وَبَيْضَةِ خِدْرٍ لَا يُرَامُ خِبَاؤُهَا

تَمَتَّعْتُ مِنْ لَهْوٍ بِهَا غَيْرَ مُعْجَلِ

تَجَاوَزْتُ أَحْرَاساً إِلَيْهَا وَمَعْشَراً

عَلَيَّ حِرَاصاً لَوْ يُسِرُّونَ مَقْتَلِي

إِذَا مَا الثُّرَيَّا فِي السَّمَاءِ تَعَرَّضَتْ

تَعَرُّضَ أَثْنَاءِ الْوِشَاحِ الْمُفَصَّلِ

فَجِئْتُ وَقَدْ نَضَتْ لِنَوْمٍ ثِيَابَهَا

لَدَى السِّتْرِ إِلَّا لِبْسَةَ الْمُتَفَضِّلِ

فَقَالَتْ يَمِينَ الله مَا لَكَ حِيلَةٌ

وَمَا إِنْ أَرَى عَنْكَ الْغَوَايَةَ تَنْجَلِي

خَرَجْتُ بِهَا أَمْشِي تَجُرُّ وَرَاءَنَا

عَلَى أَثَرَيْنَا ذَيْلَ مِرْطٍ مُرَحَّلِ

فَلَمَّا أَجَزْنَا سَاحَةَ الْحَيِّ وَانْتَحَى

بِنَا بَطْنُ خَبْتٍ ذِي حِقَافٍ عَقَنْقَلِ

هَصَرْتُ بِفَوْدَيْ رَأْسِهَا فَتَمَايَلَتْ

عَلَيَّ هَضِيمَ الْكَشْحِ رَيَّا الْمُخَلْخَلِ

مُهَفْهَفَةٌ بَيْضَاءُ غَيْرُ مُفَاضَةٍ

تَرَائِبُهَا مَصْقُولَةٌ كَالسَّجَنْجَلِ

تَصُدُّ وَتُبْدِي عَنْ أَسِيلٍ وَتَتَّقِي

بِنَاظِرَةٍ مِنْ وَحْشِ وَجْرَةَ مُطْفِلِ

Fair too was that other, she the veil-hidden one, howdahed
how close, how guarded! Yet did she welcome me.

Passed I twixt her tent-ropes, – what though her near-of-
kin lay in the dark to slay me, blood-shedders all of them.

Came I at the mid-night, hour when the Pleiades showed as
the links of seed-pearls binding the sky's girdle.

Stealing in, I stood there. She had cast off from her every
robe but one robe, all but her night-garment.

Tenderly she scolded: What is this stratagem? Speak, on
thine oath, thou mad one. Stark is thy lunacy.

Passed we out together, while she drew after us on our twin
track to hide it, wise, her embroideries,

Fled beyond the camp-lines. There in security dark in the
sand we lay down far from the prying eyes.

By her plaits I wooed her, drew her face near to me, won to
her waist how frail-lined, hers of the ancle-rings.

Fair-faced she – no redness – noble of countenance, smooth
as of glass her bosom, bare with its necklaces.

Coyly she withdraws her, shows us a cheek, a lip, she a
gazelle of Wújra, – yearling the fawn with her.

وَجِيدٍ كَجِيدِ الرِّئْمِ لَيْسَ بِفَاحِشٍ
إِذَا هِيَ نَصَّتْهُ وَلَا مُعَطَّلِ

وَفَرْعٍ يَزِينُ الْمَتْنَ أَسْوَدَ فَاحِمٍ
أَثِيثٍ كَقِنْوِ النَّخْلَةِ الْمُتَعَثْكِلِ

غَدَائِرُهُ مُسْتَشْزِرَاتٌ إِلَى الْعُلَا
تَضِلُّ الْعِقَاصُ فِي مُثَنًّى وَمُرْسَلِ

وَكَشْحٍ لَطِيفٍ كَالْجَدِيلِ مُخَصَّرٍ
وَسَاقٍ كَأُنْبُوبِ السَّقِيِّ الْمُذَلَّلِ

وَتُضْحِي فَتِيتُ الْمِسْكِ فَوْقَ فِرَاشِهَا
نَؤُومُ الضُّحَى لَمْ تَنْتَطِقْ عَنْ تَفَضُّلِ

وَتَعْطُو بِرَخْصٍ غَيْرِ شَثْنٍ كَأَنَّهُ
أَسَارِيعُ ظَبْيٍ أَوْ مَسَاوِيكُ إِسْحِلِ

تُضِيءُ الظَّلَامَ بِالْعِشَاءِ كَأَنَّهَا
مَنَارَةُ مُمْسَى رَاهِبٍ مُتَبَتِّلِ

إِلَى مِثْلِهَا يَرْنُو الْحَلِيمُ صَبَابَةً
إِذَا مَا اسْبَكَرَّتْ بَيْنَ دِرْعٍ وَمِجْوَلِ

وَلَيْلٍ كَمَوْجِ الْبَحْرِ أَرْخَى سُدُولَهُ
عَلَيَّ بِأَنْوَاعِ الْهُمُومِ لِيَبْتَلِي

فَقُلْتُ لَهُ لَمَّا تَمَطَّى بِصُلْبِهِ
وَأَرْدَفَ أَعْجَازًا وَنَاءَ بِكَلْكَلِ

أَلَا أَيُّهَا اللَّيْلُ الطَّوِيلُ أَلَا انْجَلِ
بِصُبْحٍ وَمَا الْإِصْبَاحُ مِنْكَ بِأَمْثَلِ

18

Roe-like her throat slender, white as an áriel's, sleek to thy
lips up-lifted, – pearls are its ornament.

On her shoulders fallen thick lie the locks of her, dark as the
dark date-clusters hung from the palm-branches.

See the side-plaits pendent, high on the brows of her,
tressed in a knot, the caught ones fast with the
fallen ones.

Slim her waist, – a well-cord scarce has its slenderness.
Smooth are her legs as reed-stems stripped at a
water-head.

The morn through she sleepeth, musk-strewn in indolence,
hardly at noon hath risen, girded her day dresses.

Soft her touch, – her fingers fluted as water-worms, sleek as
the snakes of Thóbya, tooth-sticks of 'Ishali.

Lighteneth she night's darkness, ay, as an evening lamp
hung for a sign of guidance lone on a hermitage.

Who but shall desire her, seeing her standing thus, half in
her childhood's short frock, half in her woman's robe!

Dim the drear night broodeth, – veil upon veil let down,
dark as a mad sea raging, tempting the heart of me.

Spake I to Night stoutly, while he, a slow camel, dragged
with his hind-feet halting, – gone the forehand of him.

Night! I cried, thou snail Night, when wilt thou turn to day?
When? Though in sooth day's dawning worse were than
thou to me.

Sluggard Night, what stays thee? Chained hang the stars
of thee fast to the rocks with hempen ropes set
un-moveable.

فَيَا لَكَ مِنْ لَيْلٍ كَأَنَّ نُجُومَهُ

بِكُلِّ مُغَارِ الْفَتْلِ شُدَّتْ بِيَذْبُلِ

كَأَنَّ الثُّرَيَّا عُلِّقَتْ فِي مَصَامِهَا

بِأَمْرَاسِ كَتَّانٍ إِلَى صُمِّ جَنْدَلِ

وَقِرْبَةِ أَقْوَامٍ جَعَلْتُ عِصَامَهَا

عَلَى كَاهِلٍ مِنِّي ذَلُولٍ مُرَحَّلِ

وَوَادٍ كَجَوْفِ الْعَيْرِ قَفْرٍ قَطَعْتُهُ

بِهِ الذِّئْبُ يَعْوِي كَالْخَلِيعِ الْمُعَيَّلِ

فَقُلْتُ لَهُ لَمَّا عَوَى إِنَّ شَأْنَنَا

قَلِيلُ الْغِنَى إِنْ كُنْتَ لَمَّا تَمَوَّلِ

كِلَانَا إِذَا مَا نَالَ شَيْئاً أَفَاتَهُ

وَمَنْ يَحْتَرِثْ حَرْثِي وَحَرْثَكَ يُهْزِلِ

وَقَدْ أَغْتَدِي وَالطَّيْرُ فِي وُكُنَاتِهَا

بِمُنْجَرِدٍ قَيْدِ الْأَوَابِدِ هَيْكَلِ

مِكَرٍّ مِفَرٍّ مُقْبِلٍ مُدْبِرٍ مَعًا

كَجُلْمُودِ صَخْرٍ حَطَّهُ السَّيْلُ مِنْ عَلِ

كُمَيْتٍ يَزِلُّ اللَّبْدُ عَنْ حَالِ مَتْنِهِ

كَمَا زَلَّتِ الصَّفْوَاءُ بِالْمُتَنَزِّلِ

عَلَى الذَّبْلِ جَيَّاشٍ كَأَنَّ اهْتِزَامَهُ

إِذَا جَاشَ فِيهِ حَمْيُهُ غَلْيُ مِرْجَلِ

مِسَحٍّ إِذَا مَا السَّابِحَاتُ عَلَى الْوَنَى

أَثَرْنَ الْغُبَارَ بِالْكَدِيدِ الْمُرَكَّلِ

Water-skins of some folk – ay, with the thong of them laid
     on my nága's wither – borne have I joyfully,
Crossed how lone the rain-ways, bare as an ass-belly;
     near me the wolf, starved gamester, howled to his
     progeny.
Cried I: Wolf, thou wailest. Surely these lives of ours, thine
     and my own, go empty, robbed of prosperity.
All we won we leave here. Whoso shall follow us, seed in our
     corn-track casting, reap shall he barrenness.

Rode I forth at day-dawn – birds in their nests asleep – stout
     on my steed, the sleek-coat, him the game-vanquisher.
Lo, he chargeth, turneth, – gone is he – all in one, like to a
     rock stream-trundled, hurled from its eminence.
Red-bay he, – his loin-cloth chafing the ribs of him
     shifts as a rain-stream smoothing stones in a river-bed.
Hard is he, – he snorteth loud in the pride of him, fierce as a
     full pot boiling, bubbling beneath the lid.
Straineth he how stoutly, while, as spent fishes swim, tied to
     his track the fleet ones plough his steps wearily.

يُزِلُّ الْغُلامَ الْخِفَّ عَنْ صَهَوَاتِهِ
وَيُلْوِي بِأَثْوَابِ الْعَنِيفِ الْمُثَقَّلِ

دَرِيرٍ كَخُذْرُوفِ الْوَلِيدِ أَمَرَّهُ
تَتَابُعُ كَفَّيْهِ بِخَيْطٍ مُوَصَّلِ

لَهُ أَيْطَلا ظَبْيٍ وَسَاقَا نَعَامَةٍ
وَإِرْخَاءُ سِرْحَانٍ وَتَقْرِيبُ تَتْفُلِ

ضَلِيعٌ إِذَا اسْتَدْبَرْتَهُ سَدَّ فَرْجَهُ
بِضَافٍ فُوَيْقَ الْأَرْضِ لَيْسَ بِأَعْزَلِ

كَأَنَّ عَلَى الْمَتْنَيْنِ مِنْهُ إِذَا انْتَحَى
مَدَاكَ عَرُوسٍ أَوْ صَلايَةَ حَنْظَلِ

كَأَنَّ دِمَاءَ الْهَادِيَاتِ بِنَحْرِهِ
عُصَارَةُ حِنَّاءٍ بِشَيْبٍ مُرَجَّلِ

فَعَنَّ لَنَا سِرْبٌ كَأَنَّ نِعَاجَهُ
عَذَارَى دَوَارٍ فِي مُلاءٍ مُذَيَّلِ

فَأَدْبَرْنَ كَالْجَزْعِ الْمُفَصَّلِ بَيْنَهُ
بِجِيدٍ مُعَمٍّ فِي الْعَشِيرَةِ مُخْوَلِ

فَأَلْحَقَنَا بِالْهَادِيَاتِ وَدُونَهُ
جَوَاحِرُهَا فِي صَرَّةٍ لَمْ تُزَيَّلِ

فَعَادَى عِدَاءً بَيْنَ ثَوْرٍ وَنَعْجَةٍ
دِرَاكاً وَلَمْ يَنْضَحْ بِمَاءٍ فَيُغْسَلِ

فَظَلَّ طُهَاةُ اللَّحْمِ مِنْ بَيْنِ مُنْضِجٍ
صَفِيفَ شِوَاءٍ أَوْ قَدِيرٍ مُعَجَّلِ

See, in scorn he casteth youth from the back of him, leaveth
    the horseman cloakless, naked the hard-rider.
As a sling-stone hand-whirled, so is the might of him,
    loosed from the string that held it, hurled from the
    spliced ribbon.
Lean his flanks, gazelle-like, legs as the ostrich's; he like a
    strong wolf trotteth; lithe as a fox-cub he.
Stout his frame; behind him, look, you shall note of him
    full-filled the hind-leg gap, tail with no twist in it.
Polished, hard his quarters, smooth as the pounding-stone
    used for a bridegroom's spices, grind-slab of colocynth.
As the henna juice lies dyed on a beard grown hoar, so on his
    neck the blood-stains mark the game down-ridden.
Rushed we on the roe-herd. Sudden, as maids at play
    circling in skirts low-trailing, forth leaped the does of it.
Flashing fled they, jewels, shells set alternately on a young
    gallant's neck-string, his the high pedigreed.
Yet he gained their leaders, far while behind him lay
    bunched in a knot the hindmost, ere they fled
    scatterwise.
'Twixt the cow and bull herds held he in wrath his road;
    made he of both his booty, – sweatless the neck of him.
All that day we roasted, seethed the sweet meat of them, row
    upon row in cauldrons, firelighters all of us.

وَرُحْنَا يَكَادُ الطَّرْفُ يَقْصُرُ دُونَهُ

مَتَى مَا تَرَقَّ الْعَيْنُ فِيهِ تَسَفَّلِ

قَبَاتَ عَلَيْهِ سَرْجُهُ وَلِجَامُهُ

وَبَاتَ بِعَيْنِي قَائِماً غَيْرَ مُرْسَلِ

أَصَاحِ تَرَى بَرْقًا أُرِيكَ وَمِيضَهُ

كَلَمْعِ الْيَدَيْنِ فِي حَبِيٍّ مُكَلَّلِ

يُضِيءُ سَنَاهُ أَوْ مَصَابِيحُ رَاهِبٍ

أَمَالَ السَّلِيطَ بِالذُّبَالِ الْمُفَتَّلِ

قَعَدْتُ لَهُ وَصُحْبَتِي بَيْنَ ضَارِجٍ

وَبَيْنَ الْعُذَيْبِ بَعْدَ مَا مُتَأَمَّلِي

عَلَى قَطَنٍ بِالشَّيْمِ أَيْمَنُ صَوْبِهِ

وَأَيْسَرُهُ عَلَى السِّتَارِ فَيَذْبُلِ

فَأَضْحَى يَسُحُّ الْمَاءَ حَوْلَ كُتَيْفَةٍ

يَكُبُّ عَلَى الْأَذْقَانِ دَوْحَ الْكَنَهْبَلِ

وَمَرَّ عَلَى الْقَنَانِ مِنْ نَفَيَانِهِ

فَأَنْزَلَ مِنْهُ الْعُصْمَ مِنْ كُلِّ مُنْزَلِ

وَتَيْمَاءَ لَمْ يَتْرُكْ بِهَا جِذْعَ نَخْلَةٍ

وَلَا أُطُماً إِلَّا مَشِيدًا بِجَنْدَلِ

كَأَنَّ ثَبِيرًا فِي عَرَانِينِ وَبْلِهِ

كَبِيرُ أُنَاسٍ فِي بِجَادٍ مُزَمَّلِ

كَأَنَّ ذُرَا رَأْسِ الْمُجَيْمِرِ غُدْوَةً

مِنَ السَّيْلِ وَالْغُثَّاءِ فَلْكَهُ مِغْزَلِ

Nathless home at night-fall, he in the fore-front still.
   Where is the eye shall bind him? How shall it follow him?
The night through he watcheth, scorneth him down to lay,
   close, while I sleep, still saddled, bridled by side of me.

Friend, thou seest the lightning. Mark where it wavereth,
   gleameth like fingers twisted, clasped in the cloud-rivers.
Like a lamp new-lighted, so is the flash of it, trimmed by a
   hermit nightly pouring oil-sésame.
Stood I long a watcher, twin-friends how dear with me, till
   in Othéyb it faded, ended in Dáriji.
By its path we judged it: rain over Káttan is; far in Sitár it
   falleth, streameth in Yáthboli.
Gathereth gross the flood-head dammed in Kutéyfati.
   Woe to the trees, the branched ones! Woe the kanáhboli!
El Kanáan hath known it, quailed from the lash of it. Down
   from their lairs it driveth hot-foot the ibexes.
Known it too hath Téyma; standeth no palm of her
   there, nor no house low-founded, – none but her
   rock-buildings.
Stricken stood Thabíra whelmed by the rush of it, like an
   old chief robe-folded, bowed in his striped mantle.
Nay, but he Mujéymir, tall-peaked at dawn of day, showed
   like a spinster's distaff tossed on the flood-water.

وَأَلْقَى بِصَحْرَاءِ الْغَبِيطِ بَعَاعَهُ

نُزُولَ الْيَمَانِي ذِي الْعِيَابِ الْمُحَمَّلِ

كَأَنَّ مَكَاكِيَّ الْجِوَاءِ غُدَيَّةً

صُبِحْنَ سُلَافاً مِنْ رَحِيقٍ مُفَلْفَلِ

كَأَنَّ السِّبَاعَ فِيهِ غَرْقَى عَشِيَّةً

بِأَرْجَائِهِ الْقُصْوَى أَنَابِيشُ عُنْصُلِ

Cloud-wrecked lay the valley piled with the load of it, high
    as in sacks the Yemámi heapeth his corn-measures.
Seemed it then the song-birds, wine-drunk at sun-rising,
    loud through the valley shouted, maddened with
    spiceries,
While the wild beast corpses, grouped like great bulbs
    up-torn cumbered the hollow places, drowned in the
    night-trouble.

عَفتِ الدِّيارُ مَحَلُّها فَمُقامُها

بمنًى تَأَبَّدَ غَوْلُها فَرِجَامُها

فَمَدَافِعُ الرَّيَّانِ عُرِّيَ رَسْمُها

خَلَقاً كما ضَمِنَ الوُحِيَّ سِلامُها

دِمَنٌ تَجَرَّمَ بَعْدَ عَهْدِ أَنِيسِها

حِجَجٌ خَلَوْنَ حَلالُها وحرامُها

رُزِقَتْ مَرابِعَ النُّجُومِ وَصابَها

وَدْقُ الرَّواعِدِ جَوْدُها فَرِهامُها

من كلِّ سارِيَةٍ وَغَادٍ مُدْجِنٍ

وَعَشِيَّةٍ مُتَجَاوِبٍ إِرْزامُها

فعلا فُرُوعُ الأَيْهَقَانِ وَأَطْفَلَتْ

بالجلهتيْنِ ظِباؤُها ونَعامُها

وَالعينُ عاكفةٌ على أَطْلائِها

عُوذاً تأجَّل بالفَضاءِ بِهامُها

وجَلا السيُولُ عنِ الطُّلولِ كأنّها

زُبُرٌ تجِدُّ مُتونَها أَقْلامُها

أوْ رَجْعُ واشمةٍ أُسِفَّ نَؤُورُها

كِفَفاً تعرّضَ فَوْقَهنَّ وِشامُها

فوقفْتُ أسألُها وكَيفَ سُؤَالُنا

صُمًّا خَوالِدَ مَا يَبِينُ كَلامُها

MU'ALLAQA

Gone are they the lost camps, light flittings, long
    sojournings in Miná, in Gháula, Rijám left how desolate.
Lost are they. Rayyán lies lorn with its white torrent beds,
    scored in lines like writings left by the flood-water.
Tent-floors smooth, forsaken, bare of all that dwelt in them,
    years how long, the war-months, months too of peace-
    pleasures.
Spots made sweet with Spring-rains fresh-spilled from the
    Zodiac, showers from clouds down-shaken, wind-wracks
    and thunder-clouds;
Clouds how wild of night-time, clouds of the dawn
    darkening, clouds of the red sunset, – all speak the
    name of her.

Here, in green thorn-thickets, does bring forth how
    fearlessly; here the ostrich-troops come, here too the
    antelopes.
Wild cows, with their wild calf-sucklings, standing over
    them, while their weanlings wander wide in the bare
    valleys.
Clean-swept lie their hearth-stones, white as a new
    manuscript writ with texts fresh-graven, penned by
    the cataracts,
Scored with lines and circles, limned with rings and
    blazonings, as one paints a maid's cheek point-lined
    in indigo.

29

عَرِيثٌ وَكانَ بها الجميعُ فَأَبْكَرُوا

منها وغُودِرَ نُؤْيُها وثُمامُها

شاقَتْكَ ظُعْنُ الحيِّ حينَ تَحَمَّلوا

فتكنَّسُوا قُطْناً تَصِرُّ خِيامُها

من كلِّ مَحْفوفٍ يُظِلُّ عِصِيَّه

زوجٌ عليهِ كِلَّةٌ وقِرامُها

زُجَلاً كَأَنَّ نِعاجَ تُوضِحَ فَوقها

وظِباءَ وَجْرَةَ عُطَّفاً آرامُها

حُفِزَتْ وَزايلها السَّرابُ كَأَنَّها

أَجْزَاعُ بِيشةَ أَثْلُها ورِضامُها

بل ما تذكَّرُ مِنْ نَوَارَ وقَدْ نَأَتْ

وتقطَّعتْ أَسْبابُهَا وَرِمامُها

مُرِّيَّةٌ حلَّتْ بِفَيْدَ وَجاوَرَتْ

أَهْلَ الحِجازِ فأيْنَ مِنكَ مَرامُها

بمشارِقِ الْجَبَلينِ أوْ مُحَجَّرٍ

فتضمَّنَتْها فَرْدَةٌ فَرُخامُها

فصُوائقٌ إِنْ أَيمنتْ فَمِظِنَّةٌ

فيها وِحافُ القَهْرِ أَوْ طِلْخامُها

فأقْطَعْ لُبانةَ مَنْ تعرَّضَ وَصْلُهُ

وَلَخَيْرُ واصِلِ خُلَّةٍ صَرَّامُها

All amazed I stood there. How should I make questionings?
    Dumb the rocks around me, silent the precipice,
Voices lost, where these dwelt who at dawn abandoning
    tent and thorn-bush fencing fled to the wilderness.
Now thy sad heart acheth, grieveth loud remembering girls
    how closely howdahed, awned with what canopies.
Every howdah curtained, lined with gauze embroideries,
    figured with festoons hung red from the pole of it.
Trooped they there the maid-folk, wild white cows of
    Túdiha, ay, or does of Wújra, long-necked, their fawns
    with them,
Fled as the miráge flees, fills the vale of Bíshata, fills the
    tree-clad wádies, íthel and rock-mazes.

What of her, Nowára, thy lost love, who fled from
    thee, every heart-link sundered, close loop and free fetter!
Hers the Mórra camp-fires lit how far in Fáïda, in Hejáz
    what marches! How shalt thou win to her?
Eastward move they marching, to Muhájjer wandering
    camped in Tái, in Férda, ay, in Rukhám of it.
Southward on to Yémen, to Sowéyk their sojournings,
    to Waháf el Káhri, ay, and Tilkhám of it.
Man, have done! forget her, – one too far to comfort thee!
    Who would his love garner first let him sunder it.

وَأَحْبُ المُجامِلَ بالجَزيلِ وَصَرْمُهُ

باقٍ إذا ظَلَعَتْ وزاغَ قِوامُها

بِطَليح أَسْفارٍ تَرَكْنَ بَقِيَّةً

مِنها فَأَحْنَقَ صُلْبُها وَسَنامُها

وإذَا تَغالَى لَحْمُها وتحسَّرَتْ

وَتَقَطَّعَتْ بَعْدَ الكَلالِ خِدَامُها

فلَها هِبابٌ في الزِّمامِ كأنَّها

صَهْباءُ خَفَّ مَعَ الجَنوبِ جَهامُها

أَوْ مُلْمِعٌ وَسَقَتْ لِأَحْقَبَ لاحَهُ

طَرْدُ الفُحولِ وَضَرْبُها وَكِدامُها

يعْلُو بها حَدَبَ الإكامِ مُسَحَّجٌ

قَدْ رابهُ عِصْيانُها وَوِحامُها

بأَحِزَّةِ الثَّلَبُوتِ يَرْبَأُ فَوْقَها

قَفْرَ المَرَاقِبِ خَوْفُها آرامُها

حتَّى إذا سَلَخا جُمادى سِتَّةً

جَزَآ فَطالَ صِيامُهُ وَصِيامُها

رَجَعا بأَمْرِهِما إلى ذِي مِرَّةٍ

حَصِدٍ وَنُجْحُ صَريمَةٍ إِبْرَامُها

وَرَمَى دَوَابِرَها السَّفا وتَهَيَّجَتْ

رِيحُ المَصَايِفِ سَوْمُها وَسَهامُها

Shed the love that fails thee. Strong be thou, and break
   with her. Keep thy gifts for friendship, freed from thy
   wilderment.
Mount thee on thy nága. Travel-trained and hard she is, low
   her back with leanness, lessened the hump of her;
Shrunk her sides and wasted, jaded with long journeyings,
   spare as her hide shoe-straps frayed by her road-faring.
Light she to her halter, to thy hand that guideth her, as a red
   cloud southwards loosed from its rain-burden.
Nay a fair wild-ass she; at her side the white-flanked one,
   he the scarred ass-stallion, bitten and struck for her.
Climbed they two the hill-top, he the bite-scarred ass-
   tyrant her new mood resenting, being in foal to him.
On the crags high posted watcheth he from Thálabut all the
   plain to guard her, ambushes laid for her.
Six months of Jumáda wandered have they waterless,
   browsing the moist herbage, he her high sentinel.
Till returned their thirsting, need of the far water clefts,
   all their will to win there speeding them waterwards.
What though with heels wounded, still the hot wind
   driveth them, as a furnace burning, fire-scorched the
   breath of it.

فَتَنازَعا سَبِطاً يَطيرُ ظِلالُهُ

كَدُخانِ مُشْعَلةٍ يُشَبُّ ضِرامُها

مشْمولةٍ غُلِثَتْ بنابِتِ عَرْفَجٍ

كَدُخانِ نارٍ ساطِعٍ أَسْنامُها

فمَضَى وَقَدَّمَها وكانَتْ عادةً

مِنْهُ إذَا هِيَ عَرَّدَتْ إقْدَامُها

فَتَوَسَّطا عُرْضَ السَّرِيِّ وَصدَّعا

مَسْجُورةً مُتجاوِراً قُلَّامها

مَحْفُوفةً وَسْطَ اليَرَاعِ يُظِلُّها

مِنْهُ مُصَرَّعُ غابةٍ وَقيامُها

أَقَتلِكَ أَمْ وَحْشِيَّةٌ مَسْبوعةٌ

خَذَلَتْ وَهادِيةُ الصَّوَارِ قِوَامُها

خَنساءُ ضَيَّعتِ الفَريرَ فَلَمْ يَرِمْ

عُرْضَ الشَّقائِقِ طَوْفُها وبُغامُها

لِمُعفَّرٍ قَهْدٍ تَنازعَ شِلْوَهُ

غُبْسٌ كَوَاسِبُ لا يُمَنُّ طَعامُها

صادفْنَ منها غِرَّةً فأَصَبْنها

إنَّ المَنايا لا تَطيشُ سِهامُها

باتَتْ وَأَسْبَلَ وَاكِفٌ من دِيمةٍ

يُرْوِي الخَمائِلَ دائماً تَسْجامُها

In their trail a dust-cloud, like a smoke it wavereth, like a
    fire new-lighted, kindling the flame of it,
Flame fanned by the North-wind, green wood mixed with
    dry fuel, smoke aloft high curling. So is the dust of them.
He, when her pace slackened, pushed her still in front of
    him. Nay, she might not falter, tyrant he urged her on,
Till they reached the streamlet, plunged and slaked their
    thirst in it, a spring welling over, crest-high the reeds
    of it;
All its banks a cane-brake, thick with stems o'ershadowing;
    bent are some, some standing, night-deep the shade of
    them.

Say is this her likeness? Or a wild cow wolf-raided of her
    sweet calf loitering, she is the van of them.
She, the short-nosed, missed it. Lows she now unendingly,
    roams the rocks, the sand-drifts, mourning and
    bellowing,
Lows in rage beholding that white shape, the limbs of it,
    dragged by the grey wolf-cubs, – who shall their
    hunger stay?
Theirs the chance to seize it, hers the short forgetfulness.
    Death is no mean archer. Mark how his arrows hit.
Stopped she then at night-fall, while the rain in long
    furrows scored the bush-grown hill-slopes, ceaseless
    the drip of it,

يَعْلو طَريقَةَ مَتْنِها مُتواتِرٌ

في لَيلةٍ كَفَرَ النُّجومَ غَمامُها

تجْتافُ أَصْلاً قالِصاً مُتَنَبِّذاً

بِعُجوبِ أَنْقاءٍ يَميلُ هَيامُها

وَتُضيءُ في وَجْهِ الظَّلامِ مُنيرَةٌ

كَجُمانةِ الْبَحْريِّ سُلَّ نِظامُها

حتّى إذا انْحَسَرَ الظَّلامُ وَأَسْفَرَتْ

بكَرَتْ تَزِلُّ عَنِ الثَّرى أَزْلامُها

عَلِهَتْ تَرَدَّدُ في نهاءِ صُعائِد

سَبْعاً تُؤاماً كامِلاً أَيّامُها

حتّى إذا يَئِسَتْ وَأَسْحَقَ حالِقٌ

لم يُبْلِهِ إرْضاعُها وَفِطامُها

فَتَوَجَّستْ رِزَّ الأَنيسِ فَراعَها

عَنْ ظَهْرِ غَيبٍ وَالأَنيسُ سَقامُها

فَغَدَتْ كِلاَ الْفَرْجَيْنِ تَحْسَبُ أَنَّه

مَوْلَى الْمَخافةِ خَلْفُها وأمامُها

حتّى إذا يَئِسَ الرُّماةُ وَأَرسَلُوا

غُضْفاً دَواجِنَ قافِلاً أَعْصامُها

فَلَحِقْنَ وَاعْتَكَرَتْ لها مَدَرِيَّةٌ

كالسَّمْهَرِيّةِ حَدُّها وتَمامُها

Dripped on her dark back-line, poured abroad abundantly:
  not a star the heaven showed, cloud-hung the pall of it;
One tree all her shelter, standing broad-branched,
  separate at the sand-hills' edge-line, steep-set the
  sides of them.
She, the white cow, shone there through the dark night
  luminous, like a pearl of deep-seas, freed from the
  string of it.
Thus till morn, till day-dawn folded back night's canopy;
  then she fled bewildered, sliding the feet of her,
Fled through the rain lakelets, to the pool Suwáyada, all a
  seven nights' fasting twinned with the days of them,
Till despaired she wholly, till her udder milk-stricken
  shrank, so full to feed him suckling or weaning him.
Voices now she hears near, human tones, they startle her,
  though to her eye naught is: Man! he, the bane of her!
Seeketh a safe issue, the forenoon through listening, now in
  front, behind now, fearing her enemy.
And they failed, the archers. Loosed they then to deal with
  her fine-trained hounds, the lop-eared, slender the sides
  of them.
These outran her lightly. Turned she swift her horns on
  them, like twin spears of Sámhar, sharp-set the points
  of them.

لِتَذُودَهُنَّ وَأَيْقَنَتْ إِن لم تَذُدْ

أَنْ قَدْ أَحَمَّ مِنَ الحُتوفِ حِمامُها

فتَقَصَّدَتْ مِنها كَسابٍ فَضُرِّجَتْ

بِدَمٍ وَغُودِرَ في المَكَرِّ سُخامُها

فَبتلْكَ إذ رَقَصَ اللَّوَامِعُ بالضُّحَى

وَأجْتابَ أرْدِيةَ السَّرابِ إِكامُها

أقضِي اللُّبانةَ لا أُفرِّطُ رِيبةً

أوْ أنْ يَلومَ بِحاجةٍ لوّامُها

أوَ لَمْ تَكُنْ تَدْري نَوارُ بأنَّني

وَصّالُ عَقْدِ حَبائلٍ جَذَّامُها

تَرّاكُ أمكنةٍ إذا لم أرْضَها

أو يَعْتَلِقْ بعضَ النُّفوسِ حِمامُها

بل أنتِ لا تَدْرِينَ كم مِنْ ليلةٍ

طَلْقٍ لذيذٍ لَهْوُها ونِدامُها

قَدْ بِتُّ سامِرَها وغايةِ تاجِرٍ

وَافَيْتُ إذْ رُفِعَتْ وَعَزَّ مُدَامُها

أغلِي السِّباءَ بكلِّ أذْكَنَ عاتِقٍ

أو جَوْنةٍ قُدِحَتْ وفُضَّ خِتامُها

بصَبوح صافيةٍ وجَذْبِ كَرِينةٍ

بمُوَتَّرٍ تأتالُهُ إبهامُها

Well she knew her danger, knew if her fence failed with
 them hers must be the red death. Hence her wrath's
 strategy.
And she slew Kasábi, foremost hound of all of them,
 stretched the brach in blood there, ay, and Sukhám
 of them.
Thus is she, my nága. When at noon the plains quiver and
 the hills dance sun-steeped, cloaked in the heat-tremors,
Ride I and my deeds do, nor forbear from wantoning, lest
 the fools should shame me, blame me the fault-finders.

Do not thou misprize me, thou Nowára. One am I binder of
 all love-knots, ay, and love's sunderer;
One who when love fails him, wails not long but flies from it;
 one whom one alone holds, hard death the hinderer.
What dost thou of mirth know, glorious nights, ah, how
 many – cold nor heat might mar them – spent in good
 company?
Came I thus discoursing to his sign, the wine-seller's drank
 at the flag-hoisting, drank till the wine grew dear,
Bidding up each full skin, – black with age the brand of it,
 pouring forth the tarred jars, breaking the seals of them;
Pure deep draughts of morning, while she played, the sweet
 singer fingering the lute-strings, showing her skill to me.

بادَرْتُ حاجتَها الدَّجاجَ بِسُحْرَةٍ
لِأُعَلَّ منها حينَ هَبَّ نِيامُها

وَغداةِ ريحٍ قَدْ وَزَعْتُ وَقِرَّةٍ
قد أَصْبَحَتْ بِيَدِ الشَّمالِ زِمامُها

ولقَدْ حَمَيْتُ الحَيَّ تَحْمِلُ شِكَّتِي
فُرُطٌ وِشاحِي إِذْ غَدَوْتُ لِجامُها

فَعَلَوْتُ مُرْتَقِياً على ذِي هَبوَةٍ
حَرِج إلى أعلامِهِنَّ قَتامُها

حتّى إذا أَلْقَتْ يَداً في كافِرٍ
وَأَجَنَّ عَوراتِ الثُّغورِ ظَلامُها

أسهلتُ وَانْتَصَبَتْ كَجِذْعِ مُنيفةٍ
جَرْداءَ يَحْصَرُ دُونَها جُرّامُها

رَفَعتُها طَرْدَ النَّعامِ وَشَلَّهُ
حتّى إذا سَخُنَتْ وخَفَّ عِظامُها

قَلِقَتْ رِحالتُها وَأَسْبَلَ نَحْرُها
وابْتَلَّ مِن زَبَدِ الحَميمِ حِزامُها

تَرْقَى وَتطعَنُ في العِنانِ وَتَنْتَحِي
وِرْدَ الحَمامةِ إِذْ أَجَدَّ حَمامُها

وَكَثيرةٍ غُرَباؤُها مجهُولةٍ
تُرْجَى نَوافِلُها وَيُخْشَى ذامُها

Ere the cock had crowed once, a first cup was quaffed by me:
    ere slow man had stretched him, gone was the second cup.
On what dawns sharp-winded clothed have I the cold with
    it, dawns that held the North-wind reined in the hands
    of them.
Well have I my tribe served, brought them aid and
    armament, slept, my mare's reins round me, night-long
    their sentinel;
Ridden forth at day-dawn, climbed the high-heaped sand-
    ridges hard by the foe's marches, dun-red the slopes
    of them;
Watched till the red sun dipped hand-like in obscurity, till
    the night lay curtained, shrouding our weaknesses;
And I came down riding, my mare's neck held loftily as a
    palm fruit-laden, – woe to the gatherer!
Swift was she, an ostrich; galloped she how wrathfully, from
    her sides the sweat streamed, lightening the ribs of her;
Strained on her her saddle; dripped with wet the neck of
    her, the white foam-flakes wreathing, edging the girth
    of her;
Thrusteth her neck forward, shaketh her reins galloping;
    flieth as the doves fly bound for the water-springs.

At the King's Court strangers thronged from what far
    provinces, each athirst for bounty, fearing indignity.

غُلب تَشَذَّرُ بالدُّخولِ كأنها

جِنُّ البَدِيِّ رَوَاسياً أَقْدَامُها

أَنكَرْتُ باطِلَها وَبُؤْتُ بِحَقِّها

عنْدِي وَلَمْ يَفْخَرْ عَلَيَّ كِرامُها

وجَزُورِ أَيْسارٍ دَعَوْتُ لِحَتْفِها

بِمَغالِقٍ مُتشَابِهٍ أَجْسامُها

أَدْعُو بهنَّ لِعاقِرٍ أَوْ مُطْفِلٍ

بُذِلَتْ لِجيرانِ الجميعِ لِحامُها

فالضَّيفُ والجارُ الجَنيبُ كأنَّما

هَبَطا تَبالةَ مُخْصِباً أَهضامُها

تأْوِي إلى الأَطْنابِ كلُّ رذِيّةٍ

مِثلِ البَلِيّةِ قالِصٍ أَهْدَامُها

ويُكلِّلونَ إذا الرِّياحُ تَناوَحَتْ

خُلْجاً تَمُدُّ شَوَارِعاً أيتامُها

إنا إذا التقَتِ المَجامِعُ لم يَزَلْ

مِنَّا لِزَازُ عظيمةٍ جشَّامُها

وَمُقَسِّمٌ يُعطِي العشيرَةَ حَقَّها

ومُغَذْمِرٌ لِحُقوقِها هَضَّامُها

فَضْلاً وَذُو كَرَمٍ يُعينُ عَلى النَّدَى

سَمْحٌ كَسوبُ رَغائبٍ غَنَّامُها

Stiff-necked they as lions in their hate, the pride of them,
    came with stubborn proud feet, Jinns of the wilderness.

Stopped I their vain boastings, took no ill-tongued words
    from them, let them not take licence. What were their
    chiefs to me?

I it was provided camels for their slaughtering, I who their
    shares portioned, drawing the lots for them.

Every mouth I feasted. Barren mount and milch-camel slew
    I for all daily. All shared the meat of them.

Far guest and near neighbour, every man rose satisfied, full
    as in Tebála, fed as in green valleys.

Ay, the poor my tent filled, thin poor souls like sick-camels,
    nágas at a tomb tied, bare-backed, no shirt on them.

Loud the winter winds howled; piled we high the
    meat-dishes; flowed the streams of fatness, feeding
    the fatherless.

Thus the tribes were trysted; nor failed we the provident to
    name one, a wise man, fair-tongued, as judge for them,

One who the spoil portioned, gave to each his just measure,
    spake to all unfearing, gave or refused to give,

A just judge, a tribe-sheykh, wise, fair-worded, bountiful,
    sweet of face to all men, feared by the warriors.

مِنْ مَعْشَرٍ سَنَّتْ لَهُمْ آباؤهُمْ
وَلِكُلِّ قَوْمٍ سُنَّةٌ وَإِمامُها

لا يَطْبَعونَ وَلَا يَبورُ فَعالُهُم
إذْ لَا يَميلُ مَعَ الهَوَى أَحْلامُها

فَأَقْنَعْ بِما قَسَمَ المَليكُ فَإِنَّما
قَسَمَ الخَلائِقَ بَيْنَنا عَلَّامُها

وإذا الأمانةُ قُسِّمَتْ في مَعْشَرٍ
أَوْفى بِأَوْفَرِ حَظِّنا قَسَّامُها

فبَنَى لَنا بيْتاً رفيعاً سَمْكُهُ
قَسَما إِلَيْهِ كَهْلُها وغُلامُها

وهُمُ السُّعاةُ إذا العَشيرةُ أُفْظِعَتْ
وهُمُ فَوارِسُها وَهُمْ حُكّامُها

وهُمُ رَبيعٌ للمُجاوِرِ فيهِمُ
والمُرْمِلاتِ إذا تَطاوَلَ عامُها

وهُمُ العشيرةُ أنْ يُبَطِّئَ حاسِدٌ
أوْ أنْ يَميلَ مَعَ العَدُوِّ لِئامُها

Noble we; our fathers wielded power bequeathed to them,
    dealt law to the nations, each tribe its lawgiver.
All our lineage faultless, no light words our promises;
    not for us the vain thoughts, passions of common men.
Thou fool foe, take warning, whatso the Lord portioneth
    hold it a gift granted, dealt thee in equity.
Loyalty our gift was, faith unstained our heritage; these fair
    things He gave us, He the distributor.
For for us a mansion built He, brave the height of it, lodged
    therein our old men, ay, and the youths of us,
All that bore our burdens, all in our tribe's sore sorrow,
    all that were our horsemen, all our high councillors.
Like the Spring are these men, joy to them that wait on
    them, to the weak, the widows, towers in adversity.
Thus our kin stands faith-firm, purged of tribe-
    malingerers. Woe be to all false friends! woe to
    the envious!

هل غادرَ الشُّعراءُ منْ متردَّمِ

أم هلْ عرفتَ الدارَ بعدَ توهمِ

يا دارَ عَبلَةَ بالجَواءِ تكلَّمي

وَعِمي صَباحاً دارَ عَبلَةَ واسلَمي

فَوَقَفتُ فيها ناقتي وَكَأَنَّها

فَدنٌ لِأَقضِيَ حاجَةَ المُتَلَوِّمِ

وَتَحُلُّ عَبلَةُ بالجَواءِ وَأَهلُنا

بالحَزنِ فَالصَمّانِ فَالمُتَثَلَّمِ

حُيِّيتَ مِن طَلَلٍ تَقادَمَ عَهدُهُ

أقوى وأقفَرَ بَعدَ أُمِّ الهَيثَمِ

حَلَّت بِأَرضِ الزائِرينَ فَأَصبَحَت

عَسِراً عَلَيَّ طِلابُكِ ابنَةَ مَخرَمِ

عُلِّقتُها عَرَضاً وَأَقتُلُ قَومَها

زَعماً لَعَمرُ أَبيكَ لَيسَ بِمَزعَمِ

وَلَقَد نَزَلتِ فَلا تَظُنّي غَيرَهُ

مِنّي بِمَنزِلَةِ المُحَبِّ المُكرَمِ

كَيفَ المَزارُ وَقَد تَرَبَّعَ أَهلُها

بِعُنَيزَتَينِ وَأَهلُنا بِالغَيلَمِ

إِن كُنتِ أَزمَعتِ الفِراقَ فَإِنَّما

زَمَّت رِكابُكُمُ بِلَيلٍ مُظلِمِ

MU'ALLAQA

How many singers before me! Are there yet songs unsung?
    Dost thou, my sad soul, remember where was her
    dwelling place?
Tents in Jiwá, the fair wádi, speak ye to me of her.
    Fair house of 'Abla my true love, blessing and joy to thee!
Doubting I paused in the pastures, seeking her camel-
    tracks, high on my swift-trotting nága tall as a citadel,
Weaving a dream of the past days, days when she dwelt in
    them, 'Abla, my true love, in Házzen, Sammán,
    Mutathéllemi.
There on the sand lay the hearth-stones, black in their
    emptiness, desolate more for the loved ones fled with
    Om Héythami,
Fled to the land of the lions, roarers importunate. Daily my
    quest of thee darkens, daughter of Mákhrami.

Truly at first sight I loved her, I who had slain her kin,
    ay, by the life of thy father, not in inconstancy.
Love, thou hast taken possession. Deem it not otherwise.
    Thou in my heart art the first one, first in nobility.
How shall I win to her people? Far in Anéyzateyn feed they
    their flocks in the Spring-time, we in the Gháïlem.
Yet it was thou, my beloved, willed we should sunder thus,
    bridled thyself the swift striders, black night
    encompassing.

ما راعَني إلّا حَمولةُ أهلِها
وَسطَ الدِيارِ تَسَفُّ حَبَّ الخِمخِمِ

فيها اثنَتانِ وَأربَعونَ حَلوبَةً
سوداً كَخافِيَةِ الغُرابِ الأسحَمِ

إذ تستبيكَ بذي غروبٍ واضحٍ
عذبٍ مقبلهُ لذيذُ المطعمِ

وكأنَّ فَارَةَ تاجرٍ بقسيمَةٍ
سبقتْ عوارضها اليكَ من الفمِ

أوْ روْضَةً أُنُفاً تضمَّن نبتَها
غيثٌ قليلُ الدِّمنِ ليسَ بمَعْلَمِ

جادَت عَليهِ كُلُّ بِكرٍ حُرَّةٍ
فَتَرَكنَ كُلَّ قَرارَةٍ كَالدِرهَمِ

سَحّاً وتسكاباً فَكلَّ عشيّةٍ
يجري عليها الماءُ لم يتصرّمِ

وَخَلا الذُبابُ بِها فَلَيسَ بِبارحٍ
غَرِداً كَفِعلِ الشارِبِ المُتَرنِّمِ

هَزِجاً يَحُكُّ ذِراعَهُ بِذِراعِه
قَدحَ المُكِبِّ عَلى الزنادِ الأجذَمِ

تمسي وتصبحُ فوق ظهرِ حشيّةٍ
وأبيتُ فوق سَراةِ ادهمَ مُلجَمِ

وحَشِيّتي سَرْجٌ على عَبْلِ الشَّوى
نَهْدٍ مَراكِلُهُ نَبيلِ المحزِمِ

Fear in my heart lay a captive, seeing their camel-herds
    herded as waiting a burden, close to the tents of them,
Browsing on berries of khímkhim, forty-two milch-camels,
    black as the underwing feathers set in the raven's wing.
Then was it 'Abla enslaved thee showing her tenderness,
    white teeth with lips for the kissing. Sweet was the taste
    of them,
Sweet as the vials of odours sold by the musk sellers,
    fragrant the white teeth she showed thee, fragrant the
    mouth of her.
So is a garden new planted fresh in its greenery, watered by
    soft-falling raindrops, treadless, untenanted.
Lo, on it rain-clouds have lighted, soft showers, no hail in
    them, leaving each furrow a lakelet bright as a silverling.
Pattering, plashing they fell there, rains at the sunsetting,
    wide-spreading runlets of water, streams of fertility,
Mixed with the humming of bees' wings droning the
    daylight long, never a pause in their chaunting, gay
    drinking-choruses.
Blithe iteration of bees' wings, wings struck in harmony,
    sharply as steel on the flint-stone, light-handed smithy
    strokes.
Sweet, thou shalt rest till the morning all the night lightly
    there, while I my red horse bestriding ride with the
    forayers.
Resting-place more than the saddle none have I, none than
    the war-horse of might in the rib-bones – deep is the
    girth of him.

                        *

هل تبلغني دارها شدنِيّة

لُعنتِ بِمَحرُوم الشَّرابِ مُصرّم

خَطّارةٌ غِبّ السُرى زَيّافةٌ

تَطِسُ الإكامَ بِوَخذِ خُفُّ ميثَمِ

وكأنّما أقصُ الإكام عشيةً

بقريبٍ بين الْمِسمين مُصلّم

تأوي له قلصُ النَّعام كما أوتْ

حِزقٌ يِمانيةٌ لأعجمَ طمطمِ

يتبعنَ قلة رأسه وكأنّهُ

حِدْجٌ على نعْشٍ لهُنَّ مخيّم

صَعلٍ يَعودُ بِذي العُشَيِرةِ بَيَضَهُ

كَالعَبدِ ذي الفَرو الطَويلِ الأصلَمِ

شَربتْ بِماءِ الدُحرُضينِ فأَصْبحتْ

زوراءَ تنفرُ عن حياض الدَّيلمِ

هِرُّ جَنيبٍ كلّما عطفتْ لهُ

غضبى اتّقاها باليدين وبالفمِ

بَرَكَتْ عَلَى جَنبِ الرِداعِ كَأَنّما

بَرَكَتْ عَلَى قَصَبٍ أَجَشَّ مُهَضَّمِ

وَكَأَنَّ رُبّاً أَو كُحَيلاً مُعقّداً

حَشَّ الوَقودُ بِهِ جَوانِبَ قُمقُمِ

يَنْباعُ مِنْ ذِفْرَى غَضوبٍ جَسرةٍ

زيافةٍ مثل الفَنيق المُكْدَمِ

50

Say, shall a swift Shadaníeh bear me to her I love, one under
ban for the drinker, weaned of the foal of her,

One with the tail carried archwise, long though the march
hath been, one with the firm foot atrample, threading the
labyrinths?

Lo, how she spurneth the sand-dunes, like to the ear-less
one, him with the feet set together; round him young
ostriches

Troop like the cohorts of Yémen, herded by 'Ajemis,
she-camel cohorts of Yémen, herded by stammerers.

Watching a beacon they follow, led by the crown of him
carried aloft as a howdah, howdah where damsels sit,

Him the small-headed, returning, fur-furnished Ethiop,
black slave, to Thu-el-Ashíra; – there lie his eggs in it.

Lo, how my nága hath drunken deeply in Dóhradeyn;
how hath she shrunk back in Déylam, pools of the
enemy.

Still to her off-side she shrinketh, deemeth the led-cat
there clawing the more that she turneth; – thus is her fear
of them.

Lo, she hath knelt in Ridá-a, pleased there and murmuring
soft as the sweet-fluting rushes crushed by the weight
of her.

Thickly as pitch from the boiling oozeth the sweat of her,
pitch from the cauldron new-lighted, fire at the sides of it,

Oozeth in drops from the ear-roots. Wrathful and bold is
she, proud in her gait as a stallion hearing the battle-cry.

*

إنْ تغدِفي دوني القناع فإنني
طبٌّ بأخذ الفارس المستلئمِ

أثني عليَّ بما علمْتِ فإنني
سمحٌ مخالقتي إذا لم أُظلَمِ

وإذا ظُلمْتُ فإنَّ ظُلميَ باسلٌ
مرٌّ مذاقتُهُ كطعم العَلقمِ

ولقد شربتُ من المدامة بعد ما
رَكَدَ الهواجرُ بالمشوفِ المُعلمِ

بزُجاجةٍ صفراءَ ذاتِ أسِرّةٍ
قرنتْ بأزهر في الشمالِ مفدَّمِ

فإذا شربتُ فإنني مُستهْلِكٌ
مالي وعرضي وافرٌ لم يُكلمِ

وإذا صَحَوْتُ فما أُقصِّرُ عنْ ندىً
وكما عَلمتِ شمائلي وَتَكَرُّمي

وحليلِ غانيةٍ تركتُ مجدَّلاً
تَمكو فريصتُهُ كشدْقِ الأعْلمِ

سبقتْ يدايَ له بعاجلِ طعنةٍ
ورشاش نافذةٍ كلوْنِ العَنْدَمِ

هَلّا سألتِ الخَيلَ يا ابنَةَ مالكِ
إن كُنتِ جاهلةً بما لم تَعلَمي

إذ لا أزالُ على رحالةِ سابحٍ
نهْدٍ تعاوَرَهُ الكُماةُ مُكَلَّمِ

Though thou thy fair face concealest still in thy veil
  from me, yet am I he that hath captured horse-riders
  how many!
Give me the praise of my fair deeds. Lady, thou knowest
  it, kindly am I and forbearing, save when wrong
  presseth me.
Only when evil assaileth, deal I with bitterness; then am
  I cruel in vengeance, bitter as colocynth.

Sometime in wine was my solace. Good wine, I drank of it,
  suaging the heat of the evening, paying in white money,
Quaffing in goblets of saffron, pale-streaked with ivory, hard
  at my hand their companion, the flask to the left of me.
Truly thus bibbing I squandered half my inheritance; yet
  was my honour a wide word. No man had wounded it.
Since that when sober my dew-fall rained no less generous:
  thou too, who knowest my nature, thou too be bountiful!
How many loved of the fair ones have I not buffeted, youths
  overthrown! Ha, the blood-streams shrill from the veins
  of them.
Swift-stroke two-handed I smote him, thrust through the
  ribs of him; forth flowed the stream of his life-blood red
  as anemone.
Ask of the horsemen of Málek, O thou his progeny, all
  they have seen of my high deeds. Then shalt thou learn
  of them
How that I singly among them, clad in war's panoply, stout
  on my war-horse the swift one charged at their chivalry.

طَوْراً يجَرِّدُ للطعانِ وتارةً

أوي الى حصدِ القسيِّ عَرَمْرَم

يُخبِرك من شَهدَ الوقيعَةَ أنني

أغشى الوغى وأعفُّ عند المغنم

ومُدجّج كَرِهَ الكماةُ نِزَالَهُ

لا مُمعن هَرَباً ولا مُستَسلم

جادتْ له كفي بعاجل طعنةٍ

مِنَثَّفِ صَدْقِ الكُعُوبِ مُقَوَّم

فَشَككتُ بالرُمح الأَصَمَّ ثِيابَهُ

لَيسَ الكَريمُ عَلى القَنا مُحَرَّم

فتركتهُ جزرَ السباع يَنُشْنَهُ

يقضمنَ حسنَ بنانهِ والمعصم

وَمشَكِّ سابغةٍ هَتكتُ فروجَها

بالسيف عن حامي الحقيقة معلم

ربذٍ يداهُ بالقداح إذا شتا

هتَّاك غايات التجار ملوَّم

لما رآني قَدْ نَزَلْتُ أُريدُهُ

أبدى نواجذهُ لغير تبسُّم

عهدي به مَدَّ النهار كأنَّما

خُضِبَ اللُّبان ورأسهُ بالعظلَم

فطعنتهُ بالرُمح ثم علوته

بمهنِّدٍ صافي الحديدة مِخذَم

54

Lo, how he rusheth, the fierce one, singly in midst of them,
    waiting anon for the archers closing in front of us.
They that were nearest in battle, they be my proof to thee
    how they have quailed at my war-cry, felt my urbanity.
Many and proud are their heroes, fear-striking warriors,
    men who nor flee nor surrender, yielding not easily.
Yet hath my right arm o'erborne them, thrust them aside
    from me, laid in their proud backs the long spear, –
    slender the shaft of it.
See, how it splitteth asunder mail-coat and armouring; not
    the most valiant a refuge hath from the point of it.
Slain on the ground have I left him, prey to the lion's brood,
    feast of the wrists and the fingers. Ha, for the sacrifice!

Heavy his mail-coat, its sutures, lo, I divided them piercing
    the joints of the champion; brave was the badge of him.
Quick-handed he with the arrows, cast in the winter-time,
    raider of wine-sellers' sign-boards, blamed as a prodigal.
He, when he saw me down riding, making my point at him,
    showed me his white teeth in terror, nay, but not
    smilingly.
All the day long did we joust it. Then were his finger tips
    stained as though dipped in the íthlem, dyed with the
    dragon's blood,
Till with a spear-thrust I pierced him, once and again with
    it, last, with a blade of the Indies, fine steel its tempering,
Smote him, the hero of stature, tall as a tamarisk, kinglike,
    in sandals of dun hide, noblest of all of them.

بَطَلٍ كَأَنَّ ثِيابَهُ في سَرحَةٍ

يُحذى نِعالَ السِبتِ لَيسَ بِتَوْأَمِ

يَا شَاةَ ما قَنَصٍ لِمَنْ حَلَّتْ لَهُ

حَرُمَتْ عليَّ وليتها لم تحرُمِ

فَبَعَثْتُ جاريتي فقلتُ لها اذْهبي

فَتَجسَّسي أخبارَها ليَ واعلمي

قالتْ رأيتُ مِنْ الأعادي غِرَّةً

والشاةُ مُمكِنةٌ لِمَنْ هُو مُرتَمِ

وكأنما التفتتْ بِجيدِ جدايةٍ

رَشَاءٍ مِن الغِزْلانِ حُرٍّ أرْثَمِ

نُبِّئتُ عَمراً غَيرَ شاكِرٍ نِعمَتي

وَالكُفرُ مَخبَثَةٌ لِنَفْسِ المُنعِمِ

ولقد حفظتُ وصاةَ عمّي بالضّحى

إذ تقلصُ الشَّفتانِ عنْ وضحِ الفمِ

في حومةِ الحربِ التي لا تشتكي

غَمَرَاتِها الأبطالُ غَيرَ تَغَمْغُمِ

إذْ يتَّقُون بي الأسَّنة لم أخِمْ

عنها ولكنّي تضايق مُقْدَمي

لما رأيتُ القومَ أقبلَ جمعهُم

يتذَامرونَ كَرَرْتُ غَيرَ مذَمَّمِ

يدعون عنترَ والرِّماحُ كأنها

أشطانُ بئرٍ في لبانِ الأدهَمِ

Oh, thou, my lamb, the forbidden! prize of competitors,
    why did they bid me not love thee? why art thou veiled
    from me?
Sent I my hand-maiden spy-like: Go thou, I said to her,
    bring me the news of my true love, news in veracity.
Go. And she went, and returning: These in unguardedness
    sit, and thy fair lamb among them, waiting thy archery.
Then was it turned she towards me, fawn-necked in
    gentleness, noble in bearing, gazelle-like, milk-white
    the lip of it.

Woe for the baseness of 'Amru, lord of ingratitude!
    Verily thanklessness turneth souls from humanity.
Close have I kept to the war-words thy father once spoke
    to me, how I should deal in the death-play, when lips part
    and teeth glitter,
When in the thick of the combat heroes unflinchingly cry in
    men's ears their defiance, danger forgot by them.
Close have I kept them and stood forth their shield from the
    enemy, calling on all with my war-cries, circling and
    challenging.
There where the horsemen rode strongest I rode out in
    front of them, hurled forth my war-shout and charged
    them; – no man thought blame of me.
Antar! they cried; and their lances, well-cords in
    slenderness, pressed to the breast of my war-horse still
    as I pressed on them.

ما زلتُ أرميهمْ بثغرةِ نحرِه

ولبانِه حتى تَسَرْبلَ بالدَّمِ

فازورَّ من وقعِ القنا بلبانِه

وشكا إليَّ بعَبْرةٍ وَتَحمْحُمِ

لَو كانَ يَدري ما المُحاوَرَةُ اشتكى

وَلَكانَ لَو عَلِمَ الكَلامَ مُكَلِّمي

ولقد شفى نفسي وأبرأ سُقمَها

قيلُ الفوارسِ ويكَ عنترَ أقدمِ

والخيلُ تقْتَحِمُ الخَبارَ عوابساً

من بين شيْظمةٍ وآخر شيْظمِ

ذلِّ ركابي حيثُ شئتُ مشايعي

لُبِّي وأحفزُهُ بِأمرٍ مُبْرَمِ

ولقد خشيتُ بأنْ اموتَ ولم تدرْ

للحربِ دائرةٌ على ابْنَي ضَمْضَمِ

الشاتِمِيْ عِرْضي ولم أشتِمْهُما

والنَّاذِرَيْنِ إذا لم ألقهما دَمي

إن يفعلاَ فلقد تركتُ أباهما

جزرَ السباعِ وكلِّ نسرٍ قشْعَمِ

Doggedly strove we and rode we. Ha, the brave stallion!
   now is his breast dyed with blood-drops, his star-front
   with fear of them!
Swerved he, as pierced by the spear-points. Then in his
   beautiful eyes stood the tears of appealing, words
   inarticulate.
If he had learned our man's language, then had he called to
   me: if he had known our tongue's secret, then had he
   cried to me.

Thus to my soul came consoling; grief passed away from it
   hearing the heroes applauding, shouting: Ho, Antar, ho!
Deep through the sand-drifts the horsemen charged with
   teeth grimly set, urging their war-steeds, the strong-
   limbed, weight bearers all of them.
Swift the delúls too I urged them, spurred by my eagerness
   forward to high deeds of daring, deeds of audacity.
Only I feared lest untimely drear death should shorten me
   e'er on the dark sons of Démdem vengeance was filled
   for me.
These are the men that reviled me, struck though I struck
   them not, vowed me to bloodshed and evil or e'er
   I troubled them.
Nay, let their hatred o'erbear me! I care not. The sire of
   them slain lies for wild beasts and vultures. Ha! for
   the sacrifice!

أَتَانِي طَيْفُ عَبْلَةَ فِي المَنَامِ

فَقَبَّلَنِي ثَلاثاً فِي اللَّثَامِ

وَوَدَّعَنِي فَأَوْدَعَنِي لَهِيباً

أُسَتِّرُهُ وَيَشْعُلُ فِي عِظَامِي

وَلَوْلَا أَنَّنِي أَخْلُو بِنَفْسِي

وَأُطْفِي بِالدُّمُوعِ جَوَى غَرَامِي

لَمُتُّ أَسَى وَكَمْ أَشْكُو لأَنِّي

أَغَارُ عَلَيْكِ يَا بَدْرَ التَّمَامِ

أَيَا ابْنَةَ مَالِكٍ كَيْفَ التَّسَلِّي

وَعَهْدُ هَوَاكِ مِنْ عَهْدِ الفِطَامِ

وَكَيْفَ أَرُومُ مِنكِ القُرْبَ يَوْماً

وَحَوْلَ خِبَاكِ آسَادُ الأَجَامِ

وَحَقَّ هَوَاكِ لَا دَاوَيْتُ قَلْبِي

بِغَيْرِ الصَّبْرِ يَا بِنْتَ الكِرَامِ

إِلَى أَنْ أَرْتَقِي دَرَجَ المَعَالِي

بِطَعْنِ الرُّمْحِ أَوْ ضَرْبِ الحُسَامِ

'ABLA'S SPIRIT

'Abla's spirit appeared to me in my sleep, and thrice I kissed her within her veil.

It bade me adieu, but it deposited in me a flame that I feel burning through my bones.

Were I not left in solitude, and could I not quench the fire of my passion with tears, my heart would melt.

But I do not complain; though all my fears are on thy account, O thou perfect full moon!

O daughter of Malik! how can I be consoled, since my love for thee originated from the time I was weaned?

But how can I ever hope to approach thee, whilst the lions of the forest guard thy tent?

By the truth of my love for thee, my heart can never be cured but by patience.

O thou noble maid! till I exalt myself to the heights of glory with the thrusts of my spear, and the blows of my sword, I will expose myself to every peril wherever the spears clash in the battle-dust – then shall I be either tossed upon the spear-heads, or be numbered among the noble.

TRANS. TERRICK HAMILTON

أَقِيمُوا بَنِي أُمِّي صُدُورَ مَطِيِّكُمْ
فَإِنِّي إِلَى قَوْمٍ سِوَاكُمْ لَأَمْيَلُ

فَقَدْ حُمَّتِ الْحَاجَاتُ وَاللَّيْلُ مُقْمِرٌ
وَشُدَّتْ لِطِيَّاتٍ مَطَايَا وَأَرْحُلُ

وَلِي دُونَكُمْ أَهْلُونَ سِيدٌ عَمَلَّسٌ
وَأَرْقَطُ زُهْلُولٌ وَعَرْفَاءُ جَيْأَلُ

هُمُ الْأَهْلُ لَا مُسْتَوْدَعُ السِّرِّ ذَائِعٌ
لَدَيْهِمْ وَلَا الْجَانِي بِمَا جَرَّ يُخْذَلُ

وَكُلٌّ أَبِيٌّ بَاسِلٌ غَيْرَ أَنَّنِي
إِذَا عَرَضَتْ أُولَى الطَّرَائِدِ أَبْسَلُ

وَإِنْ مُدَّتِ الْأَيْدِي إِلَى الزَّادِ لَمْ أَكُنْ
بِأَعْجَلِهِمْ إِذْ أَجْشَعُ الْقَوْمِ أَعْجَلُ

وَمَا ذَاكَ إِلَّا بَسْطَةٌ عَنْ تَفَضُّلٍ
عَلَيْهِمْ وَكَانَ الْأَفْضَلَ الْمُتَفَضِّلُ

وَإِنِّي كَفَانِي فَقْدَ مَنْ لَيْسَ جَازِيًا
بِنُعْمَى وَلَا فِي قُرْبِهِ مُتَعَلَّلُ

L-POEM OF THE ARABS

Get ye up, O sons of my mother, the return of your beasts from their watering; for verily I am eagerly inclined (to be off) to a set, other than you.

For matters (to look after) have sprung up; and the night is bright with the moon. The beasts, too, and the saddles, are ready girded for expeditions.

And I have (other) familiars besides you; – a fierce wolf, and a sleek spotted (leopard), and a long-maned hyæna.

They are a family with whom the confided secret is not betrayed; neither is the offender thrust out for that which has happened.

And each one (of them) is vehement in resistance, and brave; only, that I, when the first of the chased beasts present themselves, am (still) braver.

And if hands are stretched forth towards the provisions, I am not the most hasty of them. For the greediest of a party is the most hasty.

And that is naught but a stretch of (my) generosity, out of a kindness towards them. And the more excellent is he who confers a favour.

And verily, there will compensate to me the loss of whomsoever requites not a benefit, or is unmindful of its proximity,

ثَلَاثَةُ أَصْحَابٍ فُؤَادٌ مُشَيَّعٌ
وَأَبْيَضُ إِصْلِيتٌّ وَصَفْرَاءُ عَيْطَلُ

هَتُوفٌ مِنَ ٱلْمُلْسِ ٱلْمُتُونِ تَزِينُهَا
رَصَائِعُ قَدْ نِيطَتْ إِلَيْهَا وَمِحْمَلُ

إِذَا زَلَّ مِنْهَا ٱلسَّهْمُ أَنَّتْ كَأَنَّهَا
مُرَزَّأَةٌ ثَكْلَى تَرِنُّ وَتُعْوِلُ

لَعَمْرُكَ مَا بِٱلْأَرْضِ ضِيقٌ عَلَى ٱمْرِءٍ
سَرَى رَاغِبًا أَوْ هَارِبًا وَهْوَ يَعْقِلُ

وَفِي ٱلْأَرْضِ مَنْأًى لِلْكَرِيمِ عَنِ ٱلْأَذَى
وَفِيهَا لِمَنْ خَافَ ٱلْقِلَى مُتَحَوَّلُ

وَلَسْتُ بِمِهْيَافٍ يُعَشِّي سَوَامَهُ
مُجَدَّعَةً سُقْبَانُهَا وَهْيَ بُهَّلُ

وَلَا جَبَّاءَ أَكْهَى مُرِبٍّ بِعِرْسِهِ
يُطَالِعُهَا فِي أَمْرِهِ كَيْفَ يَفْعَلُ

وَلَا خَرِقٍ هَيْقٍ كَأَنَّ فُؤَادَهُ
يَظَلُّ بِهِ ٱلْمُكَّاءُ يَعْلُو وَيَسْفُلُ

وَلَا خَالِفٍ دَارِيَّةٍ مُتَغَزِّلِ
يَرُوحُ وَيَغْدُو دَاهِنًا يَتَكَحَّلُ

Three companions; – a dauntless heart, and a trenchant drawn sword, and a slimly-long yellow (bow)

That twangs loudly; of those with smooth flat surfaces, ornamented with clasps passed on to it, and a suspensory,

Which, when the arrow glides forth from it, moans, as though it were a bereaved (mother) robbed of her child, who lifts up her voice and weeps aloud.

By thy life! There is no straitness in the land for a man who journeys by night, seeking or shunning, he being wise;

And in the land (there is) a refuge from molestation for the noble-minded. And therein, for him who fears enmity, (there is) a place towards which to turn.

And I am not one impatient of thirst, who pastures his free-grazing she-camels by night, their young male colts being driven away, while they themselves are left with their dugs free;

Nor a faint-hearted poltroon who cleaves to his bride, and consults her in his matter in hand, as to how he shall manage;

Nor a terrified scare-crow, whose heart is, as it were, as though a mock-bird were therein, mounting and descending;

Nor a stay-at-home, who never quits the tent; but flirts with the women; who is occupied, evening and morning, with anointing himself and tingeing his eyes with *stibium*;

وَلَسْتُ بِعِلِّ شَرُّهُ قَبْلَ خَيْرِهِ

أَلَفُّ إِذَا مَا رُعْتَهُ اهْتَاجَ أَعْزَلُ

وَلَسْتُ بِمِحْيَارِ الظَّلَامِ إِذَا انْتَحَتْ

هُدَى الْهَوْجَلِ الْعَصِيفِ يَهْمَاءُ هَوْجَلُ

إِذَا الْأَمْعَزُ الصَّوَّانُ لَاقَى مَنَاسِمِي

تَطَايَرَ مِنْهُ قَادِحٌ وَمُفَلَّلُ

أُدِيمُ مِطَالَ الْجُوعِ حَتَّى أُمِيتَهُ

وَأَضْرِبُ عَنْهُ الذِّكْرَ صَفْحاً فَأَذْهَلُ

وَأَطْوِي عَلَى الْخُمْصِ الْحَوَايَا كَمَا انْطَوَتْ

خُيُوطَهُ مَارِيٌّ تُغَارُ وَتُفْتَلُ

وَأَسْتَفُّ تُرْبَ الْأَرْضِ كَيْلَا يَرَى لَهُ

عَلَيَّ مِنَ الطَّوْلِ امْرُؤٌ مُتَطَوَّلُ

وَلَوْ لَا اجْتِنَابُ الذَّأْمِ لَمْ يُلْفَ مَشْرَبٌ

يُعَاشُ بِهِ إِلَّا لَدَيَّ وَمَأْكَلُ

وَلَكِنْ نَفْساً مُرَّةً لَا تُقِيمُ بِي

عَلَى الضَّيْمِ إِلَّا رَيْثَمَا أَتَحَوَّلُ

وَلَا تَزْدَهِي الْأَطْمَاعُ حِلْمِي وَلَا أُرَى

سَؤُولاً بِأَعْقَابِ الْأَحَادِيثِ يَنْمُلُ

And I am not a good-for-nothing, whose ill precedes his good deed; – a drowsy-head, who starts when thou scarest him; who wears no weapon;

And I am not one bewildered by the darkness when my huge she-camel takes the direction of the trackless waste.

When the hard flint meets my hoof-like digits, there fly from it the fire-striking and the shivered fragments.

I make perpetual the term of delay for the satisfaction of the calls of hunger, until I kill it. I then turn away from noticing it, and I forget it.

And I twist my intestines about my inanition, as the yarns of a spinner are twisted when spun and laid.

And I lick up the dry dust of the earth, lest some pretender to generosity should imagine in himself a superiority over me (by offering food).

And were it not for (my) shunning what might be blamed, there would not be found, to subsist on, a potable or edible thing, excepting with me.

But (I possess) an unyielding spirit, that will not be quiet with me under a wrong, save while I turn over (in my mind what to do).

And covetings turn not to giddiness my sobriety; nor am I seen inquisitively prying at the heels of occurrences (or, news).

وَأُعْدِمُ أَحْيَاناً وَأَغْنَى وَإِنَّمَا

يَنَالُ ٱلْغِنَى ذُو ٱلْبُغْيَةِ ٱلْمُتَبَذِّلُ

وَلَا جَزِعٌ مِنْ خَلَّةٍ مُتَكَشِّفُ

وَلَا مَرِحٌ تَحْتَ ٱلْغِنَى أَتَحَيَّلُ

وَأَغْدُو عَلَى ٱلْقُوتِ ٱلزَّهِيدِ كَمَا غَدَا

أَزَلُّ تَهَادَاهُ ٱلتَّنَائِفُ أَطْحَلُ

غَدَا طَاوِياً يُعَارِضُ ٱلرِّيحَ هَافِياً

يَجُوبُ بِأَذْنَابِ ٱلشِّعَابِ وَيَعْسُلُ

فَلَمَّا لَوَاهُ ٱلْقُوتُ مِنْ حَيْثُ أَمَّهُ

دَعَا فَأَجَابَتْهُ نَظَائِرُ نُحَّلُ

مُهَلَّلَةٌ شِيبُ ٱلْوُجُوهِ كَأَنَّهَا

قِدَاحٌ بِكَفَّيْ يَاسِرٍ تَتَقَلْقَلُ

أَوِ ٱلْخَشْرَمُ ٱلْمَبْعُوثُ حَثَّتْ دَبْرَهُ

مَحَابِيضُ أَرْسَاهُنَّ سَامٍ مُعَسِّلُ

مُهَرَّتَةٌ فُوهٌ كَأَنَّ شُدُوقَهَا

شُقُوقُ ٱلْعِصِيِّ كَالِحَاتٌ وَبُسَّلُ

فَضَجَّ وَضَجَّتْ بِٱلْبَرَاحِ كَأَنَّهَا

وَإِيَّاهُ نُوحٌ فَوْقَ عَلْيَاءَ ثُكَّلُ

And I become poor at times, and (then) rich. For verily, the entertainer of desire, who does not spare himself, obtains opulence.

And I am not a repiner in poverty, habitually parading (my need); nor an exulter, proudly assuming, under wealth.

And I go forth early, upon the most frugal fare; as the dun-coloured, lean-haunched (wolf) goes forth, which deserts direct, the one to the other.

He goes forth betimes, fasting; he questions the wind, hungrily; he traverses the outlets of the passes; and skulks along with hanging head and straddling steps.

Then, when sustenance fails him, where he had sought to obtain it, he cries aloud; and his fellows, lean also, respond;

Thin as laths, hoary-faced ones, who are, as it were, (from attenuation), so many gaming arrows shuffling about in the two hands of a distributer by lot of the joints of a slaughtered camel;

Or, (as though he were) an excited queen-bee, whose swarm the spatulæ have roused up, thrust in (to their hive) by a honey-seeking hunter;

Open-jawed, wide-mouthed, as though their cheeks were splinters of staves; morose-looking, and determined.

Then he howls, and they howl, in the wide waste; as though they and he were bereaved ones, lamenting upon some high place.

وَأَغْضَى وَأَغْضَتْ وَآتَّسَى وَآتَّسَتْ بِهِ
مَرَامِيلُ عَزَّاهَا وَعَزَّتْهُ مُرْمِلُ

شَكَا وَآشْتَكَتْ ثُمَّ آرْعَوَى بَعْدُ وَآرْعَوَتْ
وَلَلصَّبْرُ إِنْ لَمْ يَنْفَعِ ٱلشَّكْوُ أَجْمَلُ

وَفَاءَ وَفَاءَتْ بَادِرَاتٍ وَكُلُّهَا
عَلَى نَكَظٍ مِمَّا تَكَاتَمَ مُجْمِلُ

وَتَشْرَبُ أَسَارِي ٱلْقَطَا ٱلْكُدْرُ بَعْدَمَا
سَرَتْ قَرَبًا أَحْنَاؤُهَا تَتَصَلْصَلُ

هَمَمْتُ وَهَمَّتْ وَآبْتَدَرْتُ وَأَسْدَلَتْ
وشمَّرَ مِنِّي فَارِطٌ مُتَمَهِّلُ

فَوَلَّيْتُ عَنْهَا وَهْيَ تَكْبُو لِعَقْرِهِ
يُبَاشِرُهُ مِنْهَا ذُقُونٌ وَحَوْصَلُ

كَأَنَّ وَغَاهَا حَجْرَتَيْهِ وَحَوْلَهُ
أَخَامِيمُ مِنْ سَفْرِ ٱلْقَبَائِلِ نُزَّلُ

تَوَافَيْنَ مِنْ شَتَّى إِلَيْهِ فَضَمَّهَا
كَمَا ضَمَّ أَذْوَادَ ٱلْأَصَارِيمِ مَنْهَلُ

فَعَبَّتْ غِشَاشًا ثُمَّ مَرَّتْ كَأَنَّهَا
مَعَ ٱلْفَجْرِ رَكْبٌ مِنْ أُحَاظَةَ مُجْفِلُ

And he becomes quiet, and they become quiet; and he imitates, and they imitate him; provisionless wanderers, whom he consoles, and who console him, he wandering provisionless.

He complains, and they complain; then, he refrains at last, and they refrain. And verily, patience, if complaint avail not, is more seemly!

And he goes back; and they go back in all haste; and all of them are busily intent on what the decent one keeps secret.

And the cinereous sandgrouse birds drink my leavings, after they have travelled a whole night, their sides audibly panting (with thirst and fatigue);

I strive, and they strive; and I quicken my pace, and they lag behind; and a leisurely harbinger, in me, has thus been allowed to tuck up his skirts;

Then I turn back from them; and they tumble over at its margin, which their chins and breasts embrace;

As though their tumult, on each side of, and round about it, (were that of) congregations settling down from migrating tribes

Coming to it from divers quarters; so that it collects them, as one watering-place collects the camel-troops of various tent-groups.

So they sip a scanty turbid puddle. Then they pass on, as though they were a caravan hasting away from Uhātza with the dawn.

وَيَوْمٍ مِنَ ٱلشِّعْرَى يَذُوبُ لُعَابُهُ

أَفَاعِيهِ فِي رَمْضَائِهِ تَتَمَلْمَلُ

نَصَبْتُ لَهُ وَجْهِي وَلَا كِنَّ دُونَهُ

وَلَا سِتْرَ إِلَّا ٱلْأَتْحَمِيُّ ٱلْمُرَعْبَلُ

وَضَافٍ إِذَا هَبَّتْ لَهُ ٱلرِّيحُ طَيَّرَتْ

لَبَائِدَ عَنْ أَعْطَافِهِ مَا تُرَجَّلُ

بَعِيدٌ بِمَسِّ ٱلدُّهْنِ وَٱلْفَلْيِ عَهْدُهُ

لَهُ عَبَسٌ عَافٍ عَنِ ٱلْغُسْلِ مُحْوِلُ

فَإِمَّا تَرَانِي كَٱبْنَةِ ٱلرَّمْلِ ضَاحِياً

عَلَى رِقَّةٍ أَحْفَى وَلَا أَتَنَعَّلُ

فَإِنِّي لَمَوْلَى ٱلصَّبْرِ أَجْتَابُ بَزَّهُ

عَلَى مِثْلِ قَلْبِ ٱلسَّمْعِ وَٱلْحَزْمُ أَفْعَلُ

طَرِيدُ جِنَايَاتٍ تَيَاسَرْنَ لَحْمَهُ

عَقِيرَتُهُ لِأَيِّهَا حُمَّ أَوَّلُ

وَأَلْفُ هُمُومٍ لَا تَزَالُ يَعُودُهُ

عِيَادًا كَحُمَّى ٱلرِّبْعِ بَلْ هِيَ أَثْقَلُ

إِذَا وَرَدَتْ أَصْدَرْتُهَا ثُمَّ إِنَّهَا

تَثُوبُ فَتَأْتِي مِنْ تُحَيْثُ وَمِنْ عَلُ

And on a day of (the canicular period of) Sirius, when his gossamer floats melting about, and his vipers, among his over-heated rocks, writhe in agony,

I set up my face right against it, with no screen in front thereof, and no covert, save a tattered At-hamī rag,

And a shaggy head of hair, on which when the wind blows, there fly out, as fluffs from its tufts, what might be combed away;

Far, in time, from the touch of oil, and from a riddance of vermin; soiled with filth; excused from washing; dishevelled.

And if thou see me, like an antelope of the sands, exposed to the sun on scanty fare, I go barefoot, and I wear no sandals.

For verily, I am a slave to patience. I wear its armour over the like of the heart of the wolf-hyæna; and discretion I practise.

(I am a man) persecuted by assaults that imperil life and limb, and that gamble on his flesh as against his death shriek, – which of them is destined to be first had;

And a familiar of cares, which cease not to revisit him, returning like the quartan ague; nay, which are yet heavier to bear.

When they beset me, I drive them away. Then, verily, they spring round, and come upon me from a little below, and from just above.

وَخَرْقٍ كَظَهْرِ التُّرْسِ قَفْرٍ قَطَعْتُهُ

بِعَامِلَتَيْنِ بَطْنُه لَيْسَ يُعْمَلُ

فَأَلْحَقْتُ أُولَاهُ بِأُخْرَاهُ مُوفِياً

عَلَى قُنَّةٍ أُقْعِي مِرَارًا وَأَمْثُلُ

وَآلَفُ وَجْهَ الْأَرْضِ عِنْدَ افْتِرَاشِهَا

بِأَهْدَأَ تُنْبِيهِ سَنَاسِنُ قَحَّلُ

وَأَعْدَلَ مَنْحُوضاً كَأَنَّ فُصُوصَهُ

كِعَابٌ دَحَاهَا لَاعِبٌ فَهْيَ مُثَّلُ

تَرُودُ الْأَرَاوِي الصُّحْمُ حَوْلِي كَأَنَّهَا

عَذَارَى عَلَيْهِنَّ الْمُلَاءُ الْمُذَيَّلُ

وَيَرْكُدْنَ بِالْآصَالِ حَوْلِي كَأَنَّنِي

مِنَ الْعُصْمِ أَدْفَى يَنْتَمِي الْكِيحَ أَعْقَلُ

وَلَيْلَةِ نَحْسٍ يَصْطَلِي الْقَوْسَ رَبُّهَا

وَأَقْطُعَهُ اللَّاتِي بِهَا يَتَنَبَّلُ

دَعَسْتُ عَلَى غَطْشٍ وَبَغْشٍ وَصُحْبَتِي

سُعَارٌ وَأَرْزِيزٌ وَوَجْرٌ وَأَفْكَلُ

فَأَيَّمْتُ نِسْوَاناً وَأَيْتَمْتُ أُلْدَةً

وَعُدْتُ كَمَا أَبْدَأْتُ وَاللَّيْلُ أَلْيَلُ

And in a wilderness, (bare) as the back of a shield, which I have traversed, the hither and thither portions of the interior of which are not usually travelled through,

The beginnings of which I have brought together with its endings (by journeying); mounting on a hill-top, to sit down at times; and (again) standing up erect (on the out-look for foes).

And I snuggle to the face of the earth, where it spreads out level, on a crooked back, built up by fleshless vertebral processes;

And on a scraggy arm, the articulations of which are, as it were, dice thrown by a player, they thus standing out erect.

The dusky chamois does wandering around me, as though they were maidens on whom are train-trailing mufflers;

And of evenings resting around me, as though I were, of the white fore-shanked ones, a long-horned chamois buck, with crooked hind legs, bound for the mountain slopes.

And in a night of wretchedness, when the owner burns his (very) bow, and his fragments (thereof), from which he could make arrows,

I tramp forth in the dark and the drizzle; my companions being heart-burning, and sleet, and rancour, and shivering.

Then I make widows of women, and I make orphans of children (in one tent); and I repeat (in other tents) as I began; the night being (still) most obscure.

وَأَصْبَحَ عَنِّي بِالْغُمَيْصَاءِ جَالِسًا

فَرِيقَانِ مَسْؤُولٌ وَآخَرُ يَسْأَلُ

وَقَالُوا لَقَدْ هَرَّتْ بِلَيْلٍ كِلَابُنَا

فَقُلْنَا أَذِئْبٌ عَسَّ أَمْ عَسَّ فُرْعُلُ

فَلَمْ تَكُ إِلَّا نَبْأَةٌ ثُمَّ هَوَّمَتْ

فَقُلْنَا قَطَاةٌ رِيعَ أَمْ رِيعَ أَجْدَلُ

فَإِنْ يَكُ مِنْ جِنٍّ لَأَبْرَحَ طَارِقاً

وَإِنْ يَكُ إِنْساً مَا كَهَا الْإِنْسُ يَفْعَلُ

فَإِنْ تَبْتَئِسْ بِالشَّنْفَرَى أُمُّ قَسْطَلٍ

لَمَا اغْتَبَطَتْ بِالشَّنْفَرَى قَبْلُ أَطْوَلُ

تَنَامُ إِذَا مَا نَامَ يَقْظَى عُيُونُهَا

حِثَاثاً إِلَى مَكْرُوهِهِ تَتَغَلْغَلُ

And on the morrow, at Gumaysā, two parties of men arose to a sitting posture (conversing together) about me (in reality), – the one being questioned and the other inquiring.

And they said (to one another): 'In the night our dogs growled; so we said: "Is a wolf prowling, or is it a hyæna-cub skulking about?"

'But it was nothing, only a slight sound; then they dozed off again; so we said: "Was it a sandgrouse got scared, or did some hawk take fright?"

'Now, if it was one of the genii, verily, he has wrought a dreadful deed! And if it was a human being, . . . ! – But what human being could do it?'

Well! If the mother of Qastel is (now) in despair through Shanfarà, verily, the advantage over Shanfarà for which she was envied, was of longer duration!

She sleeps whenever he sleeps; but her eyes (her spies are) awake as she dozes, exercising her utmost (thoughts) in what may wreak misery on him.

أَرِقْتُ لِضَوْءِ بَرْقٍ في نَشاصِ

تَلَأْلَأَ في مُمَلَّأَةِ غِصَاصِ

لِواقِعَ دُلَّحٍ بالماءِ سُحْمِ

تَثُجُّ الْماءَ مِنْ خَلَلِ الْخَصَاصِ

سَحَابٍ ذاتِ أَسْحَمَ مُكْفَهِرٍّ

تُوحِّي الْأَرْضَ قَطْراً ذا افْتِحاصِ

تَأَلَّفَ فاسْتَوَى طَبَقاً دُكاكاً

مُحِيلاً دُونَ مَثْقَبِهِ نَوَاصِ

كَلِيلٍ مُظْلِمِ الْحَجَراتِ دَاجٍ

بَهِيمٍ أَوْ كَبحْرٍ ذِي بَوَاصِ

كَأَنَّ تَبَسُّمَ الْأَنْواءِ فِيْهِ

إِذَا ما انكلَّ عنْ لِهقٍ هُصَاصِ

وَلَاحَ بِها تَبَسُّمُ واضِحاتٍ

يَزِيْنُ صَفائِحَ الْحُورِ الْقِلاصِ

سَلِ الشُّعراءَ هلْ سَبحُوا كَسَبْحِي

بُحُورَ الشِّعْرِ أَوْ غَاصُوا مَغَاصِي

لِساني بالقريضِ وَبِالْقَوَافِي

وَبِالْأَشْعارِ أَمْهَرُ في الْغِواصِ

مِنَ الْحُوْتِ الَّذِي في لُجِّ بحْرٍ

يُجِيْدُ السَّبْحَ في اللُّجَجِ الْقِماصِ

I WATCHED THROUGH THE NIGHT

I watched through the night the flashes that lit the towering
    high-piled cloud-masses filled to the full, nigh bursting:
The heavily-burdened wombs of the fruitful waters,
    that spout forth rain from many a rift of blackness:
The mists built up in darkness unfathomed, rain-drops that
    carve deep caverns when they are cast to earth-ward.
The mass grew one, compact in an even surface, and poured
    forth rain in streams from its clefts, unstinted;
Like night in its gloom it swept over all the champaign,
    one blackness, or like the sea with advancing billows.
It seemed, when the lightning clove it and flashed and
    flickered, as though in the smile of rain-bringing
    constellations
One saw the white teeth flash forth in a sudden gladness
    from faces of black-eyed maidens that laugh in joyance.

Nay, ask thou the poets if they can swim as I swim the seas
    of the art of song, or can dive as I dive!
My tongue, in the shaping deftly of praise, or banning,
    and choosing of cunning words, is a nimbler swimmer
Than in the sea the fish that amid the billows swims bravely,
    and dives deep down to the depths of Ocean.

إذا ما باص لاحَ بِصَفْحَتيْهِ
وبَيَّضَ في الْمكَرِّ وفي الْمحاصِ
تُلاوِصُ في الْمَداصِ مُلاوَصَاتٌ
لهُ مَلْصَى دواجِنُ بالْمِلاصِ
بَناتُ الْماءِ لَيْس لَها حَياةٌ
إذا أخْرَجْتَهُنَّ مِن الْمَداصِ
إذا قَبَضَتْ عَلَيْهِ الْكَفُّ حيناً
تَناعَصَ تَحْتَها أيَّ انْتِعاصِ
وباصَ وَلَاصَ مِنْ مَلَصٍ مَلاصٍ
وَحوتُ الْبَحْرِ أسْودُ أوْ مِلاصِ
كَلوْنِ الْماءِ أسْودُ ذُوْ قُشُور
نُسِجْنَ تَلاحُمَ السَّرْدِ الدِّلاصِ

When he darts forward, see how his sides flash brightly,
    and how when he turns the white scales shine and glitter;
And how, on the right and left, as he swims, the watching
    shoal of small fry keep close to the smooth rocks'
    shelter –
The brood of the sea – no life have they left, if only thou
    liftest them from the wave where they dart and circle.
But he, if the hand goes forth in attempt to grasp him,
    he slips from beneath it, not to be caught with fingers!
So swims he, advancing now and retreating smoothly,
    – and black in the sea are slippery fishes ever,
The sea's own colour, guarded by scaly armour set close
    as the scales on doublets of mail well woven.

ما رَعَدَتْ رَعْدَة وَلا بَرَقَتْ

لكِنَّها أُنْشِئَتْ لَنا خَلِقَهْ

الماءُ يَجْري عَلَى نِظام لَهُ

لَوْ يَجِدُ الْماءُ مَخْرَقاً خَرَقَهْ

بِتْنا وَباتَتْ عَلَى نَمارِقِها

حَتَّى بَدَا الصُّبْحُ عَيْنُها أَرِقَهْ

أَنْ قِيلَ إِنَّ الرَّحيلَ بَعْدَ غَدٍ

والدَّارُ بَعْدَ الْجَميع مُفْتَرِقَهْ

NO THUNDER CAME

No thunder came from the cloud nor lightning flash:
    it rose and spread, giving hope to us of the rain.
The rain-drops fell from it one by one in a string –
    where water finds but a crevice, through it will fare.
We passed the night, she and I, stayed there on her rugs;
    till spread the dawning, her eyen closed not their lids,
For that 'twas said – 'After morning march we away,
    and all the folk gathered here shall scatter abroad'.

'ABID
TRANS. SIR CHARLES LYALL

ما لِذا المَوْتِ لا يَزالُ مُخيفَا

كلَّ يَوْم يَنالُ مِنّا شَريفَا

مولَعاً بالسِّراةِ مِنّا، فما يأخُذُ

إلا المُهذَّبَ الغِطْريفَا

فلو أنَّ المَنُونَ تَعْدِلُ فينَا

فتَنالُ الشَّريفَ والمشْرُوفَا

كانَ في الحقِّ أنْ يعودَ لنا المَوْتُ

وأن لا نسُومَه تَسْويفَا

أيّها المَوْتُ لو تجافَيْتَ عن صَخْرٍ

لألفيتَه نَقيّاً عَفيفَا

عاشَ خمسين حِجَّةً يُنْكِرُ المُنْكَرَ

فينا ويَبْذِلُ ألمَعْرُوفَا

رَحمةُ اللهِ والسلامُ عَليهِ

وسَقى قَبْرَهُ الرّبيعُ خَريفَا

LAMENT FOR A BROTHER

What have we done to you, death
that you treat us so,
with always another catch
one day a warrior
the next a head of state;
charmed by the loyal
you choose the best.
Iniquitous, unequalling death
I would not complain
if you were just
but you take the worthy
leaving fools for us.

Fifty years among us
upholding rights
annulling wrongs,
impatient death
could you not wait
        a little longer.
He still would be here
and mine, a brother
without a flaw. Peace
be upon him and Spring
rains water his tomb
        but
could you not wait
        a little longer
        a little longer,
you came too soon.

AL-KHANSA'

TRANS. OMAR POUND

85

لَلُبْسُ عباءةٍ وتقرّ عَيني
أحَبُّ إليَّ من لُبسِ الشفوف

وبيتٌ تخفقُ الأرْواحُ فيه
أحَبُّ إليَّ من قَصر مُنيفِ

وبِكْرٌ يتبع الأظْعان صَعْبٌ
أحَبُّ إليَّ من بَغْلٍ زفوفِ

وكلْبٌ يَنبحُ الأضْياف دوني
أحَبُّ إليَّ من هزِّ الدَّفوفِ

وخِرقٌّ من بني عَمّي فقيرٌ
أحَبُّ إليَّ من عِلْج عليفِ

SONG OF MAISUNA

The russet suit of camel's hair,
　　With spirits light and eye serene,
Is dearer to my bosom far
　　Than all the trappings of a queen.

The humble tent, and murmuring breeze
　　That whistles through its fluttering walls,
My unaspiring fancy please,
　　Better than towers and splendid halls.

Th' attendant colts, that bounding fly
　　And frolic by the litter's side,
Are dearer in Maisuna's eye
　　Than gorgeous mules in all their pride.

The watch-dog's voice, that bays whene'er
　　A stranger seeks his master's cot,
Sounds sweeter in Maisuna's ear
　　Than yonder trumpet's long-drawn note.

The rustic youth, unspoiled by art,
　　Son of my kindred, poor but free,
Will ever to Maisuna's heart
　　Be dearer, pampered fool, than thee!

MAYSUN

TRANS. J. D. CARLYLE

يا مَنْ لقلبٍ مُتَيَّم كَلِفِ

يَهْذِي بِخَوْدٍ مَرِيضةِ النَّظَرِ

تَمشي الهُوَيْنا إذا مشتْ فُضُلاً

وهْيَ كَمِثلِ العُسْلُوجِ في الشجرِ

ما زال طَرْفي يَحَارُ إذ بَرَزَتْ

حتى رأيتُ النقصانَ في بَصَري

أبصرتُها ليلةً ونِسْوَتها

يَمْشينَ بين المَقَامِ والحَجَرِ

ما إن طَمِعنا بها ولا طَمِعَتْ

حتى ٱلتقينا ليلاً على قَدَرِ

بِيضاً حِسَاناً خَرَائِداً قُطُفاً

يَمْشينَ هَوْنا كمِشْية البقرِ

يُنْصِتْنَ يوماً لها إذا نطقتْ

كَيْما يُشَرِّفْنَها على البَشَرِ

قالت لِتِرْبٍ لها تُحدِّثها

لَنُفْسِدَنَّ الطَّوافَ في عُمرِ

قُومي تَصَدَّيْ له ليعرفَنا

ثم أغمِزيه يا أخت في خَفَرِ

AH FOR THE THROES OF A HEART SORELY WOUNDED!

Ah for the throes of a heart sorely wounded!
Ah for the eyes that have smit me with madness!
Gently she moved in the calmness of beauty,
Moved as the bough to the light breeze of morning.
Dazzled my eyes as they gazed, till before me
All was a mist and confusion of figures.
Ne'er had I sought her, and ne'er had she sought me;
Fated the love, and the hour, and the meeting!
There I beheld her, as she and her damsels
Paced 'twixt the temple and outer enclosure:
Damsels the fairest, the loveliest, the gentlest,
Passing like slow-wending heifers at evening,
Ever surrounding with courtly observance
Her whom they honour, the peerless of women.
Then to a handmaid, the youngest, she whispered:
''Omar is near; let us mar his devotions.
Cross on his path that he needs may observe us;
Give him a signal, my sister, demurely.'

قالت لها قد غمزتُه فأبى

ثم ٱسْبَطَرّتْ تسعَى على أَثَرِي

من يُسْق بعد المنام ريقَتَها

يُسْق بِمسْكٍ وبارِدٍ خَصِرِ

'Signals I gave, but he marked not or heeded,'
Answered the damsel, and hasted to meet me.
He who the morn may awake to her kisses
Drinks from the cup of the blessed in heaven!

'UMAR IBN ABI RABI'A

TRANS. WILLIAM GIFFORD PALGRAVE

فلم أرَ ليلَى بعد مَوْقِفِ ساعةٍ

بخَيْفِ مِنَّى تَرمِي جِمارَ المحصَّبِ

ويُبدِي الحصَى منها إذا قَذَفتْ به

من البُرْدِ أطرافَ البَنانِ المخضَّبِ

فأصبحتُ من لَيْلَى الغَداةَ كناظرٍ

مع الصبحِ في أعقابِ نجمٍ مُغرِّبِ

أيا وَيْحَ مَنْ أمْسى تخلَّس عقلُه

فأصبح مذهوباً به كلَّ مذهبِ

خليًا من الخُلَّانِ إلا مُعذِّرا

يُضاحِكني مَنْ كان يهوَى تَجَنُّبِي

إذا ذُكِرتْ ليلى عَقلْتُ وراجعتْ

روائعُ عقلي مِن هَوًى مُتَشَعِّبِ

وقالوا صحيحٌ ما به طيفُ جِنَّةٍ

ولا الهمُّ إلا بافتراء التكذّبِ

وشاهدُ وجدي دمعُ عيني وحُبُّها

بَرَى اللحم عن أحناءِ عظمي ومنكِبِي

تجنَّبتُ ليلى أن يَلِجَّ بكَ الهوى

وهيهاتَ كان الحبُّ قبل التجنُّبِ

ألا إنَّما غادَرْتِ يا أمَّ مالكٍ

صَدًى أينما تَذْهبْ به الريحُ يَذْهبِ

I LAST SAW LAILA

I last saw Laila that Pilgrimage day
at Mina, in Mecca's stone-shot vale,
when at every cast her tunic sleeve
unsheathed long beauty signed in red,
and the dawn still found me standing there
watching the western star as it set.
What luck for one bereft of his mind,
carried away beyond all bounds,
deserted by friends of trust, though excused,
and regaled with the banter of former dislike!

At the name of Laila the senses return
as horses return from frenzied flight.
'Normal, of madness not a trace,'
they say, 'just given to fanciful talk,
affecting love by avoiding the girl.'
No, love was first, before all else,
and witness to passion are tears and tears
and the flesh that has wasted from shoulder and limb,
and nothing, O Laila, now remains
but echoes adrift on the flying wind.

تَعلّقتُ لَيْلَى وهي ذاتُ ذُؤَابةٍ
ولم يَبْدُ للأتراب من ثَدْيِها حجمُ
صغيريْن نرعَى البَهْمَ يا ليتَ أننا
إلى أليوم لم نَكْبَرْ ولم تَكْبَرِ البَهْمُ

LAILA I LOVED

Laila I loved when tresses she wore
and her gown had not yet swelled with her breast;
two children among their flocks – O why
the change! Had only the flocks stayed lambs!

MAJNUN LAYLA   95
TRANS. CHARLES GREVILLE TUETEY

أُحِبُّكَ حبّيْن حُبّ الهَوَى
وحُبّاً لأنّك أهلٌ لذاكا

فأمّا الذي هو حُبّ الهَوَى
فشُغلِي بذِكرِكَ عَمّن سِواكا

وأمّا الذي أنْتَ أهلٌ لَهُ
فكَشْفكَ لي الحُجب حتى أراكا

فلا الحَمد في ذا ولا ذاك لي
ولكن لكَ الحَمد في ذا وذاكا

TWO WAYS I LOVE THEE

Two ways I love Thee: selfishly,
 And next, as worthy is of Thee.
'Tis selfish love that I do naught
Save think on Thee with every thought;
'Tis purest love when Thou dost raise
The veil to my adoring gaze.
Not mine the praise in that or this,
Thine is the praise in both, I wis.

RABI'A AL-'ADAWIYYA   97
TRANS. R. A. NICHOLSON

يا قمراً أبْرَزَهُ مأتَمٌ،

يَنْدُبُ شَجْواً بينَ أتْرَابِ

يَبْكي فيَذْري الدُّرَّ من نرْجسٍ

ويَلْطُمُ الوَرْدَ بعُنّابِ

لا تَبْكِ مِيتاً حَلَّ في حُفْرةٍ،

وابكِ قتيلاً لكَ بالبابِ

أبْرَزَهُ المأتَمُ لي كارِهاً،

برغْمِ دايات وحُجّابِ

لا زالَ موْتاً دأبُ أحبابِهِ،

ولمْ تَزَلْ رُؤيَتُهُ دابي

O MOON CALLED FORTH BY LAMENT

O moon called forth by lament,
wailing in grief among girls,
beating roses abloom
with fingers crimson-tipped:
Cry not for the one laid out,
but for him you have killed at the gate!
Lament by force showed her off
to spite her guardians' wish.
How, but through death among hers,
shall her sight grow a custom with me?

ABU NUWAS   99
TRANS. CHARLES GREVILLE TUETEY

دَسَّتْ لهُ طيْفَها كيما تُصالحُهُ،

في النَّوْمِ حينَ تَأبَى الصُّلْحَ يقْظانَا

فلمْ يجدْ عند طَيْفي طيْفُها فرَحاً،

ولا رَنَى لتشكِّيه، ولا لانا

حسَبْتُ أنَّ خيالي لا يكونُ لَما

أكونُ من أجْلِه غَضْبانَ، غضْبانَا

جِنانُ لا تَسْأليني الصُّلْحَ مسرعةً،

فلَمْ يكنْ هيِّناً منك الّذي كانا

SHE SENT HER LIKENESS STEALING IN DREAM

She sent her likeness stealing in dream
to him who waking would not be appeased.
But her phantom found no favour with mine,
which stood its ground, unmoved by complaint.
You fancied my phantom a shade too light
anger to feel at what angers me so.
Ask not for a truce so soon, Jinân,
for the things you did were far from a dream.

ABU NUWAS

TRANS. CHARLES GREVILLE TUETEY

سَلِّمْ على ذِكْرِ الغزالِ
الأغْيَدِ المُسْبِي الدَّلالِ
سَلِّمْ عليهِ وَقُلْ لَهُ
يا غُلَّ أَلْبابِ الرِّجالِ
خَلَّيْتَ جسمي صاحِياً
وَسَكَنْتَ في ظِلِّ الْحِجالِ
وَبَلَغْتَ مِنِّي غايةً
لَمْ أَدْرِ فيها ما احتِيالي

حَقُّ الذي يَعْشَقُ نَفْسَيْنِ أنْ
يُصْلَب أو يُنشر مِنْشارِ
وعاشِقُ الْواحِدِ مِثْلُ الذي
أخْلَصَ دينَ الْواحِدِ الْباري
صَبَرْتُ حَتَّى ظَفِرَ السُّقْمُ بي
كَمْ تَصْبِرُ الحَلْفاءُ للنّارِ
لَوْلا رجائي العَطْفَ من سَيِّدي
بَقيتُ بَيْنَ الْبابِ والدّارِ

THREE LOVE EPIGRAMS

I GREETINGS TO THAT GAZELLE

Greetings to that gazelle,
  so graceful and so tempting!
Greetings to him, and say to him:
  O You who keep men's hearts enchained,
You left my body scorching in the sun
  while you live in the *shade* of women's quarters.
You've brought me to my wits' end, where
  I don't know what to do.

II WHOEVER LOVES TWO PERSONS

Whoever loves two persons should
  be crucified or sawn in twain.
But loving only one is like believing with
  one's whole heart in the One Creator.
I have endured it until sickness conquered me:
  Can halfa grass withstand the fire?
If I can't hope for his, my master's, sympathy
  I will remain as if I sat between two stools.

كَتَمْتُ اسمَ الْحَبيبِ مِن الْعِبادِ

وَرَدَّدْتُ الصَّبابة في فؤادي

فواشَوْقي إلى بلدٍ خَلِيٍّ

لَعَلِّي بِاسْمِ مَن أهْوَى أُنادي

I have hidden the name of my love from the crowd:
 for my passion my heart is the only safe space.
How I long for an empty and desolate place
 in order to call my love's name out aloud.

'ULAYYA BINT AL-MAHDI
TRANS. GEERT JAN VAN GELDER

شاب علينا أَمْرَنا شائبٌ

وقد وَددْنا أنّه لم يَشُبْ

طُوبَى لطيرٍ تَلقط الحَبَّة الـ

ـمُلقاةَ أو وَحْشٍ تَقَفَّى العُشْبْ

لا تَألَفُ الإنْسَ ولا تَعرف الـ

ـقِنْسَ ولا تسمو اليها الأُشْبْ

فلا تَشُبِّ الحربَ وقَّادةً

فخامدٌ في نفْسه من يَشُبْ

SOME POWER TROUBLED OUR AFFAIRS

Some Power troubled our affairs – and we
Had fondly wished them from his troubling free.
Blessed are birds that pick up scattered grain,
Or wild-kine seeking green sands after rain;
Strangers to man: nor they the high-born know
Nor mounts to them the infection of the low.
War's fire raise not thou to burst ablaze,
For soon in ashes sink the hands that raise.

AL–MA'ARRI

TRANS. R. A. NICHOLSON

أصبحتُ في يومي أُسائِلُ عن غدي

متحيّراً عن حاله مُتَنَدِّسا

أمّا اليقينُ فلا يقينَ وإنَّما

أقْصَى آجتهاديَ أن أَظُنَّ وأَحْدِسا

BEWILDERED

Bewildered, searching how things stand with me,
I ask to-day, 'To-morrow what shall be?'
There is no certainty: my mind but tries
Its utmost in conjecture and surmise.

AL-MA'ARRI

TRANS. R. A. NICHOLSON

أضْحَى التَنائي بَديلاً مِنْ تَدانِينَا،

وَنَابَ عَنْ طِيبِ لُقْيانَا تَجَافِينَا

أَلَا وَقد حانَ صُبْحُ البَينِ، صَبّحَنا

حَيْنٌ، فقامَ بِنَا للحَيْنِ نَاعِينَا

مَنْ مُبْلِغُ المُلْبِسِينا، بانتزَاحِهِمُ،

حُزْناً، مَعَ الدّهرِ لا يَبْلى ويُبْلِينَا

أنّ الزّمانَ الذي ما زالَ يُضْحِكُنا،

أُنْساً بقُرْبِهِمُ، قدْ عادَ يُبْكِينَا

غَيظَ العِدا مِنْ تَساقِينا الهَوَى فدعَوْا

بِأنْ نَغَضَّ، فقالَ الدّهرُ آمِينَا

POEM IN N

Morning came – the separation –
substitute for the love we shared,
for the fragrance of our coming together,
falling away.

The moment of departure
came upon us – fatal morning.
The crier of our passing
ushered us through death's door.

Who will tell them
who, by leaving, cloak us
in a sorrow not worn away with time,
though time wears us away,

That time that used
to make us laugh
when they were near
returns to make us grieve.

We poured for one another
the wine of love. Our enemies seethed
and called for us to choke
– and fate said let it be.

فانَحلَّ ما كان معقُوداً بِأَنْفُسِنَا،

وَانْبَتَّ ما كان مَوْصُولاً بِأَيْدِينَا

وَقَدْ نَكُونُ، وَما يُخشَى تَفرُّقُنا،

فاليَوْمَ نَحْنُ، ومَا يُرْجى تَلاقِينَا

يا لَيْتَ شِعري، ولم نُعتِبْ أعادِيَكم،

هَلْ نَالَ حَظّاً مِنَ العُتبَى أعادِينَا

لم نَعْتَقِدْ بَعدَكُمْ إلاّ الوَفاء لكُمْ

رَأياً، وَمْ نَتقلّدْ غَيْرَهُ دِينا

ما حَقُّنا أن تُقِرّوا عَينَ ذِي حَسَدٍ

بِنَا، وَلا أن تَسُرّوا كاشِحاً فِينَا

كُنّا نُرَى اليَأَسَ تُسلِينا عَوَارِضُه،

وَقَدْ يَئِسْنَا فمَا للِيَأس يُغْرِينَا

The knot our two souls tied
came undone,
and what our hands joined
was broken.

We never used to give a thought
to separation, and now, for us
to be together again
is beyond our dreams.

How I wish I knew –
and I have given your rivals
no satisfaction – if ours
have won a share from you.

Keeping faith in you,
now you are gone,
is the only creed we hold,
our religion.

What is our fault
that you cool the envier's eye,
satisfying one who takes
pleasure in our misfortune?

To give up hope, we thought,
might bring relief. But it only
made desire for you
burn deeper.

بِنْتُمْ وَبِنا، فما ابْتَلَّتْ جَوَانِحُنا

شَوْقاً إلَيْكُمْ، وَلا جَفَّتْ مَآقِينا

يَكادُ، حِينَ تُناجِيكُمْ ضَمائِرُنا،

يَقضي عَلَينا الأَسَى لَوْلا تَأَسِّينا

حَالَتْ لِفِقْدِكُمُ أَيّامُنا، فغَدَتْ

سُوداً، وكانتْ بِكُمْ بِيضاً لَيَالِينا

إنْ جانِبُ العَيشِ طَلْقٌ مِن تَأَلُّفِنا،

وَمَرْبَعُ اللَّهْوِ صافٍ مِنْ تَصَافِينا

وإذْ هَصَرْنا فُنُونَ الوَصْلِ دانِيَة

قِطافُها، فجَنَيْنا مِنْهُ ما شِينا

لِيُسقَ عَهدُكُمُ عَهدُ السُّرُورِ فما

كُنْتُمْ لأَرْواحِنا إلّا رَياحِينا

You left. We went our way,
ribs still scorched –
longing for you –
tears still welling in our eyes.

When our secret thought
whispered in your ear,
sorrow would have crushed us,
had we not held on to one another.

Our days turned
in losing you and darkened,
while nights with you
glowed,

When life bounded
free in the intimacy we gave,
when the meadows of our pleasure
were pure,

When whatever we wished
we gathered
from the boughs of loving
bending near.

Oh the good times spent with you –
God bless them with a gentle rain.
You were for our spirits
the fragrance of basil.

لا تَحسَبُوا نَأْيَكُمْ عَنَّا يُغَيِّرُنا،
أنْ طالَما غَيَّرَ النَّأْيُ المُحِبِّينا

واللهِ ما طَلَبَتْ أهْواؤُنا بَدَلاً
مِنْكُمْ، وَلا انصرَفَتْ عنكمْ أمانينَا

يا سارِيَ البَرْقِ غادِ القَصْرَ واسقِ به
مَنْ كان صِرْفَ الهَوى والوُدَّ يَسقينَا

واسألْ هُنالِكَ هَلْ عَنَّى تَذكُّرُنا
إلفاً، تَذكُّرُهُ أمْسَى يُعَنِّينَا

وَيا نَسِيمَ الصَّبا بَلِّغْ تَحِيَّتَنا
مَنْ لَوْ على البُعْدِ حَيّاً كان يُحيينا

فَهَلْ أرَى الدَّهرَ يَقضِينا مُساعَفَةً
مِنْهُ، وَإنْ لم يكُنْ غِبّاً تَقاضِينَا

Do not imagine
that distance from you
will change us,
as distance changes other lovers.

We sought, by God,
no other in your place,
nor do our hopes
turn us another way.

Night-traveler, lightning,
go early to the palace
and offer a drink to one
who poured us her pure love freely,

And ask if thoughts of us
trouble a lover
as the memory of her
possesses our troubled mind.

O fragrant breath of the east wind
bring greetings to one,
whose kind word would revive us
even from a distance.

Will she not, through the long
pass of time, grant us consideration,
however often, however
well we plead?

رَبِيبُ مُلكٍ، كأنَّ اللهَ أنْشَأهُ

مِسكاً، وقدّر إنشاءَ الوَرى طِينَا

أوْ صَاغَهُ وَرِقاً مَحْضاً، وَتَوَّجهُ

مِنْ نَاصِعِ التّبرِ إبْداعاً وتَحسِينَا

إذا تَأوَّدَ آدَتْهُ، رَفاهِيَةً،

تومُ العُقُودِ، وَأدمَتْهُ البُرَى لِينَا

كانَتْ لَهُ الشّمسُ ظِئْراً في أكلَته،

بَل ما تَجَلَّى لها إلاّ أَحَايِينَا

كأنّما أُثبِتَتْ، في صَحنٍ وَجنَتِهِ،

وُهْرُ الكَواكِبِ تعويذاً وَتَزْيِينَا

ما ضَرّ أنْ لمْ نَكُنْ أكفاءهُ شَرفاً،

وَفي المَودةِ كافٍ مِن تَكافِينَا؟

Fostered in royalty
as if God shaped her from musk
(and we mere humans
from clay),

Or formed her in pure silver
and crowned her
with gold, unalloyed,
new creation and glory.

When she bends,
her necklace weighs her down –
bracelets bruise her skin
so tender!

Within her veils
she is the nursling of the sun
though it touches her
barely.

As if on the curve
of her cheek, the star
of Venus were graven,
amulet and charm.

What harm is it
we are not of her station.
In love, and it is enough,
we are equal.

يا رَوْضَةً طالَمَا أُجْنَتْ لَوَاحِظَنَا

وَرْداً، جَلاهُ الصَّبا غَضّاً، وَنَسْرِينَا

وَيَا حَيَاةً تَمَلَّيْنَا، بِزَهْرَتِهَا،

مُنَى ضُرُوباً، وَلَذَّاتٍ أفانِينَا

وَيَا نَعِيماً خَطِرْنَا، مِنْ غَضَارَتِهِ،

في وَشْيِ نُعْمَى، سَحَبنا ذَيلَه حِينَا

لَسنا نُسَمِّيكِ إجْلالاً وَتَكْرِمَةً

وَقَدْرُكِ المُعْتَلي عَنْ ذاك يُغْنِينَا

إذا انفَرَدْتِ وما شُورِكتِ في صِفةٍ،

فَحَسبُنا الوَصْفُ إيضاحاً وَتَبْيِينا

يا جَنَّة الخُلدِ أُبدِلنا، بِسَلسلِها

والكَوْثَرِ العَذبِ، زَقُّوماً وغِسْلِينَا

O garden where our gazes
gathered rose and sweetbriar
unveiled soft and tender
by young amours!

O life, in whose brilliance
we were granted our wishes,
each and every kind,
drawing out our pleasure!

O the good times gone by
when we strolled in splendor,
adorned in its robes,
long folds trailing!

We cannot name you.
In station you transcend
all names, freeing us
of the obligation.

You are unique, the one and only.
Your qualities cannot be shared.
We are left to describe you
as best we can.

O garden never dying,
your lote tree and spring of Kawthar
are now for us the tree of skulls
and the drink of the damned.

كأنّنَا لم نَبِتْ، والوَصْلُ ثالِثُنَا،

وَالسّعدُ قد غَضَّ من أجفانِ وَاشِينَا

سِرّانِ في خاطِرِ الظّلماءِ يَكتُمُنا،

حتّى يَكادَ لِسانُ الصّبحِ يُفشِينَا

لا غَرْوَ في أنْ ذكرْنا الحزْنَ حينَ نهتْ

عنهُ النُّهَى، وَتركْنا الصّبرَ ناسِينَا

إنّا قرَأنا الأسَى، يوْمَ النّوَى، سُوَراً

مَكتوبَةً، وأخَذْنا الصّبرَ تَلْقِينَا

أمَا هَوَاكِ، فلَمْ نَعدِلْ بِمَنْهلِهِ

شُرْباً وَإنْ كان يُرْوِينَا فيُظْمِينَا

لمْ نَجْفُ أُفقَ جَمالٍ أنتِ كَوْكَبُهُ

سالِينَ عَنهُ، وَلم نَهجُرْهُ قالِينَا

Did we not spend the night,
making love our third companion,
when our good luck weighed
on our informer's eyes,

Two secrets
hidden in the whisper of darkness,
until the morning's tongue
was about to reveal us.

No wonder we recalled
sadness forbidden
to prudent minds,
our patience gone and forgotten.

We read our sorrow,
that dawn of parting
as Qur'an, reciting it by heart
from the verse of patience.

We can find no drink
like loving you –
even as it quenches
it leaves us thirsting more.

Nothing can divert our gaze
from the horizon
of the beauty of your star.
Bitterness cannot turn us from it.

وَلا اخْتِياراً تَجَنَّبْناهُ عَنْ كَثَبٍ،

لكِنْ عَدَتْنا، على كُرْهٍ، عَوَادِينا

نأسَى علَيكِ إذا حُثَّثْ، مُشَعْشَعَةً،

فينا الشَّمُولُ، وَغَنَّانا مُغَنِّينا

لا أكْؤسُ الرّاحِ تُبدي من شمائِلِنا

سِيما ارْتِياحٍ، وَلا الأوْتارُ تُلْهِينا

دُومي على العهدِ، ما دُمْنا، مُحافِظَةً،

فالْحُرُّ مَنْ دان إنْصافاً كما دِينا

وَلَوْ صَبا نَحْوَنَا، من عُلوِ مَطلَعِه،

بَدرُ الدُّجى لم يكنْ حاشاكِ يُصْبِينا

أبْكي وَفاءً، وَإنْ لم تَبْذُلي صِلَةً،

فالطَيفُ يُقنِعُنا، وَالذِّكْرُ يَكفِينا

Not by choice did we
withdraw from so near!
Time's twist, destiny
turned us against our will.

As the wine is mixed
and sparkles, and singers
perform their trance of song,
we ache for you.

The passing round of the cup of wine
brings out in us no mark of repose
the sound of a lute,
no forgetting.

Be true to our vow
as we have been.
The noble give back,
loyally, as given.

If from its towering course the night's
full moon bent toward us,
she would not (forgive the thought)
stir our desire.

I am left sad, keeping the faith
though you have shut
me out. A phantom
will be enough, memories suffice.

إنْ كان قد عزّ في الدّنيا اللّقاءُ بِكُم

في مَوْقِفِ الحَشرِ نَلقاكُمْ وَتَلقُونَا

وَفي الجَوَابِ مَتَاعٌ، إنْ شفعتِ به

بَيضَ الأيَادي، التي ما زِلتِ تُولِينَا

عَلَيكِ منّا سَلامُ اللهِ ما بَقِيَتْ

صَبَابَةٌ بِكِ نُخْفِيهَا، فتَخْفِينَا

Though in this world
we could not afford you,
we'll find you in the stations
of the last assembly, and pay the price.

A response from you
would be something!
If only what you offered
you gave.

God bless you
long as our love for you still burns,
the love we hide,
the love that gives us away.

IBN ZAYDUN
TRANS. MICHAEL A. SELLS

ألا هَلْ لَنا من بعد هذا التفرّقِ

سبيلٌ فيشكو كلُّ صبٍّ بما لَقِي

وقد كنتُ أوقاتَ التزاور في الشتا

أبيتُ على جمرٍ من الشوق محرقِ

فكيف وقد أمسيتُ في حالِ قطعةٍ

لقد عَجَّلَ المقدورُ ما كنتُ أتّقي

تمرُّ الليالي لا ارى البينَ ينقضي

ولا الصبرَ من رِقِّ التشوّق معتقي

سقى اللهُ أرضاً قدْ غدتْ لكَ منزلاً

بكل سَكوبٍ هاطلِ الوبل مُغْدِقِ

MUST SEPARATION MEAN WE HAVE
NO WAY TO MEET?

Must separation mean we have no way to meet?
Ay! Lovers all moan about their troubles.
For me it is a winter not a trysting time,
Crouching over the hot coals of desire.
If we're apart, nothing can be otherwise.
How soon just the very thing I feared
Was what my destiny delivered. Night after night
And separation going on and on and on,
Nor does my being patient free me from
The shackles of my longing. Please God
There may be winter rains pelting copiously down
To irrigate the earth where you now dwell.

WALLADA
TRANS. CHRISTOPHER MIDDLETON AND
LETICIA GARZA-FALCÓN

أرى روضةً قد حان منها قطافُها،
وليس يُرى جانٍ يمدُّ لها يدا
فوآ أسفي يمضي الشبابُ مضيّعاً،
ويبقى الذي ما إن اسمّيه مفرَدا

SEEING HERSELF BEAUTIFUL
AND NUBILE

I see an orchard
Where the time has come
For harvesting,
But I do not see
A gardener reaching out a hand
Toward its fruits.
Youth goes, vanishing; I wait alone
For somebody I do not wish to name.

QASMUNA BINT ISMA'IL
TRANS. CHRISTOPHER MIDDLETON AND
LETICIA GARZA-FALCÓN

أَلَا حَيِّ أَوْطَانِي بِشِلْبٍ، أَبَا بَكْرِ

وَسَلْهُنَّ هَلْ عَهْدُ الوِصَال كما أَدْرِي

وَسَلِّمْ على قصر الشَّرَاجِيب، عَنْ فَتًى

لَهُ، أَبَدًا، شَوْقٌ إلى ذَلَك القصر

مَنَازُل آسَادٍ وَبِيض نَوَاعِمٍ،

فَنَاهِيكَ مِنْ غِيلٍ، وناهِيك مِنْ خِدْرِ

وَكَمْ لَيْلَة قدْ بِتُّ أَنْعَمُ جُنْحَهَا

بِمُخْصَبَة الأَرْدَافِ مُجْدَبَة الخَصْرِ

وَبِيضٍ، وَسُمْرٍ، فاعِلَات مُهْجَتِي،

فِعَالَ الصَّفاح البِيض وَالأَسل السُّمْرِ

وَلَيْلٍ بِسُدّ النَّهْر لَهْوًا قَطَعْتُهُ

بِذَات سِوَار مِثْلَ مُنْعَطَفِ البَدْرِ

نَضَتْ بُرْدَهَا عن غُصْن بَان مُنَعَّمٍ،

نَضِير كَمَا انْشَقَّ الكِمَامُ عن الزَّهْرِ

وَبَاتَتْ تُسْقِينِي المُدَامَ بِلَحْظَهَا

فمِنْ كَأْسِهَا حِينا وَحِينا من الثَّغْرِ

وَتُطْرِبُنِي أَوْتَارُهَا وَكَأَنني

سَمِعْتُ بِأَوْتار الطُّلَى نغم البِّرِ

OF THE PLACE OF HIS YOUTH

Friend, greet at Silves many a pleasant spot
We knew, and if they recollect us not,
Say I remember them, though far away.
To Sharájíb, my palace, thou shalt say
'Greeting! The young man who saluteth thee
Longs for thy joys and thy tranquillity.'
Ah me, what nights among the sculptured halls
I dallied, where between the selfsame walls
Mingled the lion and the lithe gazelle,
Damsel and warrior; and it was well.
Sweet nights, when maidens, fair and dusky-eyed,
With looks more sharp than javelins to the side
Between their lashes, pierced me all about, –
Great was the assault and sudden was the rout!
Sweet nights, sweet nights, beneath the consummate moon
To live, and love, and plead, and crave a boon
Of kisses by the dusky river-side
From one, a singing damsel, subtle-eyed.
Fair as the image of the moon was she
Upon the lake, and fired the blood of me
With lips and looks and wondrous wine. And last
She took the painted lute, and having passed
Deft fingers o'er the strings, she played an air,
A martial air; faster and yet more fast
Thundered my blood, and clash of arms was there,
War-cries and battle-music everywhere!

And then – O sweetest moment of the night! –
Casting the girdle and the robe aside,
She stood in living beauty to my sight,
All marvellous. – 'Behold, the bud,' I cried,
'Hath broken and the flower is opened wide!'

AL-MU'TAMID
TRANS. DULCIE LAWRENCE SMITH

كتبتُ وعندي من فِراقكَ ما عِندي

وشَوقي كَمنْ قد بان عن جَنَّةِ الخُلْدِ

وما خَطَّت الأقلامُ إلَّا وأَدمُعي

تَخُطُّ سُطورَ الشَّوقِ في صَفْحَةِ الخَدِّ

ولولا طِلابُ المجدِ زُرْتُكَ طيَّهُ

عَميداً كما زارَ النّدى ورَقَ الوَرْدِ

THE LETTER

I wrote, and in my heart was burning
The grief of parting, and that yearning
They only realise
Who lose eternal paradise.

My pen no single letter traced,
But that my tears as swiftly raced
To write upon my cheek
The words my anguished heart would speak.

But for the quest of glory high
My lovesick heart were lief to fly
To thee this hour, as flows
The dew upon the waking rose.

AL-MU'TAMID

TRANS. A. J. ARBERRY

بي مِن الأقمارِ	مَعشرَ العُذّالِ
مِسْنَ في أكفالِ	أغصنٌ ميّادَهْ
كلَّ عانٍ صَبّ	قد جَنَى مِن لاما
طلعتْ في قُضْبٍ	بُبدورٍ ذاما
في هواها قلبي	مِن قدودٍ هاما
قد براها الباري	ربّةُ الخَلخالِ
هيَّجتْ بلبالي	لِعذابي غادَهْ

روحُه مَوْصولا	عَجباً للوامقْ
حيث نال السُّولا	مستهَامٌ زاهقْ
زاد فيه القِيلا	وجمالٌ رامقْ
لا يُقيم اعذاري	نَبهتْ والقالي
وهي لا ترعَى لي	شغَفي قد زادَهْ

غايةٌ لا تُدرَكُ	غايتي في الحسنِ
مثلُها قطُّ يُترك	لم يكن في عَدنِ
لحظاتٌ تَفتكُ	وُكّلتْ بحَيني
كم هِزبَرٍ ضارٍ	فَتكةَ الأبطالِ
وهُو ذو أشبالِ	سِحرُها قد صادَهْ

MUWASHSHAHA

Disparagers of love, now hear my song;
Though you be of a mind to do love wrong,
Believe me, moonlight is the stuff whereof
My lady's limbs are made. I offer proof.

Something I saw, full moon in her, alive,
Cool in her balanced body, took me captive;
Her beauty, young, her anklets, with a thrill
They pierced my heart, to cause my every ill.

A lover is a man amazed. Desire
Can drive him mad the moment he's on fire;
Heartsick, when he has had the thing he wants;
Worse, if he's deceived by what enchants.

A lover knows he's not the only one.
His lady's garden gate, she keeps it open:
A challenge – passion hurts him even more.
Whom will she choose? Whom will she ignore?

I'm of a kind a woman's body charms
So to the quick, it's Eden in her arms:
Absolute beauty being all we seek,
We can be melted by a touch of magic.

أين منها الشمسُ	أين منها البدرُ
والشفاهُ اللعسُ	زان فاها الدرُّ
ليس فيها لَبْسُ	ولماها خمرُ
ولا عن أفكاري	لم تزُلْ عن بالي
دُون ما إذلالِ	وهْي لي مُنقادَهْ

إذ شدتْ في إثرِ	أنذرَتْ بالصَّدِّ
ودموعي تجري	عَضَّ ذاك النهدِ
كانسكابِ القطرِ	تارةً في الخدِ
لا ترش موطاري	مربشي يرضا لي
بالويه وابالي	التواني عاده

As for the moon, so for the sun: from both
She draws her power; moon pearls grace her mouth,
Solar fire crimsons her lips, and yet
She's not ambiguous when her heart is set:

Burning in my reflections, day by day,
In every act of mine she has her say;
Even when, if ever, she's at peace,
You'll never find her supine in the least.

Such is my proven moon, my lady love.
Yet of myself she did once disapprove:
Pointing to the marks my teeth had made
Across her breast, then eyeing me, she said:

'Easy does it, not too quick,
I like it slow, and nothing new.
Custom knows a thing or two,
It's to custom we should stick:
Festina lente, that's the trick –
Come at me slow, I'll come with you.'

IBN QUZMAN   141
TRANS. CHRISTOPHER MIDDLETON AND
LETICIA GARZA-FALCÓN

ضاحكٌ عن جُمانْ   سافرٌ عن بَدرِ
ضَاقَ عنهُ الزمانْ   وَحَواهُ صَدْري
آه ممَّا أجِدْ   شَفَّني ما أجِدْ
قامَ بي وقعَدْ   باطشٌ مَتِّئدْ
كلما قلتُ قَدْ   قالَ لي أيْنَ قَدْ

وَانْثَنَى خُوطَ بَانْ   ذا مَهَزٍّ نَضِرِ
عابَثَتْهُ يَدَانْ   للصَّبا والقَطْرِ
لَيْسَ لي مِنْكَ بُدْ   خُذْ فُؤادي عَنْ يَدْ
لم تَدَعْ لي جَلَدْ   غير أنِّي أجْهَدْ
مَكْرَعٌ مِن شُهُدْ   وَاشْتِياقي يَشْهَدْ

ما لِبِنْتِ الدِّنانْ   ولذاكَ الثَّغْرِ
أين مُحَيّا الزَّمانْ   مِن حُمَيّا الخَمْرِ
بي هَوًى مُضْمَرُ   لَيْتَ جَهْدي وَقْفُهْ
كُلُّما يَظْهَرُ   فَفُؤَادي أُفْقُهْ
ذلك المَنْظَرُ   لا يُداوي عِشْقُهْ

MUWASHSHAHA

Laughing out of pearls, A full moon appears
Surpassing all Time Though held in my heart;
  Alas for my woe! I pine in distress!
  I danced to her tune; A gentle assailant.
  If I say: 'At last,' 'How d'you know?' says she.
She sways like a willow Green, supple, and fresh
Which is teased by the hands Of the breeze and the rain.
  I cannot resist you: Take my heart in abasement.
  A fresh spring of honey Puts an end to the patience
  Which I try to maintain; My yearning bears witness
To the daughter of jugs And to that sweet mouth.
What's the face of all Time To the flush of that wine?
  All my love I conceal, Would my efforts could end it!
  When it starts to arise, Its horizon's my heart.
  That beautiful vision Leaves my passion unhealed

فَلَكِيٌّ دُرِّي	بِأَبِي كَيْف كانْ
عُذْرُهُ وَعذْري	راقَ حتى ٱسْتَبانْ
أَوْ إلى أَنْ أَيْأَسا	هلْ إلَيْكَ سَبيلْ
عَبْرَةً أَوْ نَفَسا	ذُبْتُ إلّا قَليلْ
ساءَ ظَنِّي بِعَسى	ما عَسى أَنْ أَقولْ

وأَنا أَسْتَشْري	وَٱنْقَضَى كُلُّ شَانْ
جَزَعي أَوْ صَبْري	خالِعًا مِن عِنانْ
لَوْ تَناهَى عَنّي	ما على مَنْ يَلُومْ
دِينُهُ التَجَنّي	هَلْ سِوَى حُبِّ رِيمْ
وَهْوَ بي يُغَنّي:	أنا فيهِ أُهيمْ

أَيشْ عليك سَتَدْري	قَدْ رَأَيْتُك عِيانْ
وَسَتَنْسَى ذِكْري	سَيَطُولُ الزَّمَانْ

O, why, by my father,
Shine forth and reveal
  Is there no way to you?
  I wept not a little;
  I thought what to say;
Since all comes to nought.
I gallop loose reined,
  It harms not my blamer
  Yet for the love of a doe
  I'm possessed by despair,
'I see that you're pining;
You know Time will pass

Did a pearly bright star
Her excuse and my plea?
  Must I always despair?
  Tears flowed and I sighed;
  'Perhaps' makes me sad,
Yet am I headstrong;
Unbridling restraint.
  That she keeps avoiding,
  Whose habit's accusing
  While she sings this ditty:
I say, what's with you man;
And you will forget me.'

أَرَى شَجرَ النّارِنْجِ أَبْدى لنا جَنَّى

كقطرِ دُموعٍ ضَرَّجَتْها اللّواعِجُ

كُرَاتُ عَقيقٍ في غُصونِ زَبَرْجَدٍ

بكفِّ نسيمِ الرّيحِ مِنْها صَوالجُ

تُقَبِّلُها طَوراً وطوراً نَشُمُّها

فهنَّ خُدودٌ بَيْنَنا ونوافجُ

ORANGES

Yonder stands the orange-tree
Showing off its fruits to me,
Gleaming teardrops lovers shed
Stained by passion's heartbreak red.

Balls of agate carmine-bright
Hung on boughs of chrysolite,
Sent a-spinning from the trees
By the mallet of the breeze.

Now I kiss them, now inhale;
Thus my senses I regale
With their cheeks' so tender bloom
And the sweets of their perfume.

IBN SARA
TRANS. A. J. ARBERRY

وَمستحسنٍ عند الطّعام مُدَحْرَج

غَذاهُ نَميرُ الماءِ في كلّ بُستانِ

أطافتْ بهِ أقْماعُه فكأنّهُ

قُلوبُ نِعاجٍ في مَخاليبِ عُقبانِ

AUBERGINES

Fine to taste they are,
Smoothly globular,
Fed by the sweet brook
In their shady nook.

Fronds at top and toe
Clutch them round, as though
They are hearts of sheep
In the eagle's grip.

IBN SARA
TRANS. A. J. ARBERRY

والبَدْرُ قد ذَهب الخُسوف بِبَعضِهِ

في لَيْلَة جَزَرت أواخِرَ مَدِّها

فكأنَّهُ مِرآةُ قينٍ أُحْميت

فمشى احْمِرار النَّارِ في مُسْوَدِّهَا

MOON IN ECLIPSE

Whenas the swarming flood of night
Was ebbing from the sky
The moon, eclipsing, lost the light
Of half its eye.

The moon a blacksmith's mirror seemed
That, furnaced more and more,
Glowed, till the fiery crimson streamed
Its blackness o'er.

IBN HAMDIS
TRANS. A. J. ARBERRY

اشْرَبْ على بِركةِ نَيلوفَر

مُحْمَرّة الأوْراق خَضْراء

كأنّما أزهارُها أخرجَتْ

ألسنةَ النّارِ من الماءِ

WATER-LILIES

Drink by the pool
Where shines the beautiful
Water-lilies' sheen,
Crimson on green.

The blossoms break
The mirror of the lake,
And adroitly aim
Their tongues of flame.

IBN HAMDIS
TRANS. A. J. ARBERRY

غزَالِيَّةُ الأَلْحاظِ رِميَّةُ الطُّلى

مُدامِيَة الأَلْمى حَبابِيَّةُ الثَّغْرِ

تَرنَّحُ في مَوْشِيَةٍ ذَهِبِيَّةٍ

كما اشتبكتْ زُهرُ النُّجوم على البَدْرِ

وقد خلَعَت ليلاً عَلينا يدُ الهَوى

رداءَ عِناقٍ مَزَّقَتْهُ يدُ الفَجْرِ

LOVELY MAID

Of a lovely maid I tell:
Sombre eyes of a gazelle,
Throat of hind, and wine-red lip,
Teeth like bubbles sweet to sip.

Drunkenly she swooned and swayed
In her gown of golden braid,
Twinkling stars that interwove
Round the moon, my radiant love.

Passion's hand enveloped us
In his garment amorous
All the night, till it was torn
By the jealous hand of morn.

IBN KHAFAJA
TRANS. A. J. ARBERRY

لله نَهْرٌ سَالَ في بَطحاءِ

أشهى وُروداً من لَمى الحَسناءِ

مُتعطِف مِثل السِّوارِ كأنَّهُ

والزَّهْرُ يَكْنُفُه مَجَرَّ سَماءِ

أمَسَتْ تَحُفُّ بِه الغصونُ كأنَّها

هُدْبٌ يَحُفُّ بِمُقْلَةٍ زَرقاءِ

والرِّيحُ تَعْبَثُ بالغُصونِ وقد جرى

ذَهَبُ الأَصيْلِ عَلى لُجَيْنِ الماءِ

LOVELY RIVER

Lovely river, spread
On its stony bed,
Sweeter far to sip
Than proud beauty's lip.

Curving through the land
Like a bracelet, and
Fringed with flowers gay,
Heaven's Milky Way.

Overhanging boughs
Sweep about its brows,
Eyelashes that lie
Round an azure eye.

As the zephyrs play
The lithe branches sway:
Sunset's gorgeous beam
Gilds the silver stream.

IBN KHAFAJA
TRANS. A. J. ARBERRY

ثنائي على تلك الثنايا لأنني
أقولُ على علمٍ وأنطقُ عن خُبْرِ
وأُنصِفُها، لا أكذب الله، أنني
رَشفْتُ بها ريقاً ألَذَّ من الخمرِ

THOSE LIPS I PRAISE

Those lips I praise because I know
What I am saying, what I mean.
I do them justice, tell no lies.
From them I've drunk and what I drank
Tasted better than any wine.

HASFA BINT AL-HAJJ   159
TRANS. CHRISTOPHER MIDDLETON AND
LETICIA GARZA-FALCÓN

سلامٌ على سلمى ومَن حلَّ بالحِمى
وحُقَّ لمثلي، رِقَّةً، أن يُسلَّما

وماذا عَليها أن تَرُدَّ تحيّةً
علينا، ولكن لا احتكامَ على الدُّمَى

سَروا وظلامُ اللَّيلِ أرْخى سُدولَه
فقلت لها صَبّاً غريباً مُتيَّما

أحاطتْ به الأشواقُ صَوْناً وأُرْصِدتْ
لهُ راشقاتُ النَّبلِ أيّان يَمَّما

فأبدَتْ ثَنَاياها، وأوْمضَ بارقٌ
فلم أدرِ مَن شَقَّ الحَنَادِسَ منهُما

وقالَت أما يَكفيهِ أنّي بقَلبِهِ
يشاهدُني في كلّ وقتٍ أمَا أمَا

160

AS NIGHT LET ITS CURTAINS
DOWN IN FOLDS

Peace, Sálma, and peace
to those who halt awhile
at al-Híma. It is right
for one like me to greet you.

Would it have hurt her
to return the greeting?
Ah, but a statuette
goddess is beyond control.

They left as night
let its curtains down in folds.
I told them of a lover
strange and lost,

Surrounded by yearnings,
struck by their arrows
on target always,
wherever he goes.

She smiled, showing her side teeth.
Lightning flashed.
I couldn't tell which of the two
split the darkness.

Isn't it enough she said
I am in his heart
where each moment he sees me,
isn't it, no?

IBN AL-'ARABI

TRANS. MICHAEL A. SELLS

يا طَلَلاً عندَ الأثيلِ دارِسا

لاعبتُ فيه خُرّداً أوانِسا

بالأمسِ كان مُؤنساً وضاحِكاً

واليومَ أضحَى مُوحِشاً وعابِسا

نأوا، ولمْ أشعُرْهُمُ، فما دَرَوا

أنَّ عليهِمْ مِن ضَميري حارِسا

يَتبَعُهُم حيثُ نأوا وخيَّمُوا

وقد يكونُ للمَطايا سائِسا

حتّى إذا حلّوا بقَفْرٍ بلقَعٍ

وخَيَّمُوا، وافترَشُوا الطَّنافِسا

THE TOMBS OF THOSE WHO LOVED THEM

O windswept wasted ruin at al-Utháyl,
   where I used to play
      with young women
who knew discretion.

Yesterday it embraced us
   laughing. Today
      it frowns
in desolation.

They left without
   my knowing.
      Little did they know
my inner self could see

and follow, however far
   they journeyed, wherever
      they set their tents.
It might have been I leading their camels.

Until they halted
   in the barrenlands,
      pitched their tents
and spread their carpets.

عادَ بِهِمْ رَوْضاً أَغَنَّ يانِعاً

من بعدِ ما قدْ كان قَفْراً يابِسَا

ما نَزَلُوا من مَنزِلٍ إلّا حَوَى

من الحِسانِ رَوْضَةً طَواوِسَا

ولا نأوا عن منزلٍ إلّا حوَى

من عاشِقِيهِمْ أرضُهُ نَوَاوِسَا

They were brought back to a garden,
    wet colors singing,
        on what had been drought-split
hardened empty ground.

Whatever halt they chose
    to take their rest
        was filled with forms of beauty
like peacocks.

When they struck camp
    they left a land
        holding the tombs
of those who loved them.

هجرتُ بديعَ القولِ هَجْرَ المباينِ

فلا بالمعالي لا ولا بالمَعاينِ

وكيف أعاني سَجْعَة أو قرينة

وقد فُقِدَتْ منّي أجلُّ القرائنِ

ثوتْ في مهاوي الترِبِ كالتِبر خالصاً

فحققْتُ أنَّ الترْبَ بعض المعادنِ

فوالله ما أدري لحسنِ خلائقٍ

تسحُّ جفوني أم لخلقٍ محاسنِ

دفنْتُك يا شخص الحبيب وقد بدا

لعينك حالي قلتُ إنك دافني

كلانا على الأيّامِ باكٍ وانّما

أشدّ البلا بين الحشا كلَّ كامنِ

الى الله أشكو يوم فقدك انه

عليَّ ليوم الحشر يومُ التغابنِ

وكنتُ أخاف البين قبلك والنوى

فأصبحتُ لا آسي على اثر بائنِ

كأنك بادرْت الرحيل تخوّفاً

عليَّ من الحسن الذي هو فاتني

فديتك من لي من سناك بلمحة

وينزل بي من بعدها كلَّ كائنِ

I HAVE RENOUNCED AND GIVEN UP
ALL SPEECH SUBLIME

I have renounced and given up all speech sublime,
    no glorious deeds, no more seductive charms!
How can I bear to pair fair words in rhyme
    when I have lost the one with whom I was a pair?
She, pure as gold, rests deep down in the earth;
    I know now that the earth, too, is a precious mineral.
I don't know if it is for her sweet ways
    that I am crying, or for her sweet looks.
I've buried you, the form of my beloved: if
    you saw me, you would say you've buried me,
Each of us crying for the days gone by;
    although the keenest pain is hidden in the heart.
My grievance is with God; till Judgment Day
    the day I lost you is a Day of Fraud.
I used to be afraid of leaving before you
    and now I'm inconsolable for a departed one.
It is as if you hastened your departure, fearing that
    I'd be enamored of your beauty overmuch.
My dear one – who will grant me of your radiance
    a glance? And who can take her place?
Will I ever forget a frame thus fine, straight as
    a lance, not to be stabbed with finding faults?
Her face, which every moonlit night would favor?
    Her eyes, the talk of every fawn of a gazelle?

أأنسى قواماً أثقف الحسنُ رمحه

فما فيه من عيب يعدّ لطاعنِ

ووجهاً حكى عن حسنه كلَّ مقمر

ولحظاً روى عن طرفه كلَّ شادنِ

فوا أسفا حتّى أوسّد في الثرى

ويدني الرّدى منا مقيماً لظاعنِ

ويا ليْت شعري في القيامة هل أرى

محاسنها ما بين تلك المواطنِ

رشاقة ذاك القدّ فوق صراطه

ودينار ذاك الخدّ بين الموازنِ

سقتك غوادي المزن انيَ ظامىء

الى الترب طوعاً للزمان المحارن

شكوتُ زماناً خان بعد أحبتي

وبالغ في العدوى وبثَّ الضغائنِ

فلو طاب ليَ طابت حياتي بعدهم

وكنتُ ألاقيهم بطلعة خائنِ

Woe is me! – until the earth will be my pillow, and
   my death will bring me near to my departed one.
I wish I knew if I might see, on Resurrection Day,
   her beauties in those other habitats:
Her graceful figure on the Path to Paradise,
   her cheeks, bright as gold coins, between the Scales.
May morning rainclouds drench your grave;
   I thirst for earth, obeying stubborn Time.
My plaint is against Time the traitor, the
   aggressor who spreads malice, with my loved ones gone.
– But then again, were Time and life both good to me,
   I'd turn on my departed love a traitor's face.

IBN NUBATA AL-MISRI
TRANS. GEERT JAN VAN GELDER

وما السعادة في الدنيا سوى شبحٍ

يُرجى فإن صار جسماً ملَّهُ البشرُ

كالنهر يركض نحو السهل مكتدحاً

حتى إذا جاءَه يبطي ويعتكرُ

لم يسعد الناسُ الاَّ في تشوُّقهمْ

الى المنيع فإن صاروا به فتروا

فإن لقيت سعيداً وهو منصرفٌ

عن المنيع فقل في خُلقه العبرُ

OF HAPPINESS AND HOPE

SAGE

Happiness is a myth we seek,
  If manifested surely irks;
Like river speeding to the plain,
  On its arrival slows and murks.

For man is happy only in
  His aspiration to the heights;
When he attains his goal, he cools
  And longs for other distant flights.

If you should meet a happy one
  Who is contented with his lot,
Unlike the rest of all mankind,
  Pray his Nirvana disturb not.

ليس في الغاب رجاءٌ

لا ولا فيه المللْ

كيف يرجو الغاب جزءاً

وعلى الكل حصلْ؟

وبما السعي بغابٍ

أمَلًا وهو الأملْ؟

إنما العيش رجاءً

إحدى هاتيك العللْ

أعطني النايَ وغنِّ

فالغنا نارٌ ونورْ

وأنينُ الناي شوقٌ

لا يدانيه الفتورْ

YOUTH

Hope is found not in the forest,
    Nor the wild portray despair;
Why should forest long for portions
    When the ALL is centered there?

Should one search the forest hopeful,
    When *all nature* is the Aim?
For to hope is but an ailment,
    So are station, wealth and fame.

Give to me the reed and sing thou!
    For the song is flame and light,
And the reed's plaint is a yearning
    Unattained by lazy wight.

JIBRAN KHALIL JIBRAN   173
TRANS. GEORGE KHEIRALLAH

فإن لقيتَ محبّاً هائماً كلفاً

في جوعِهِ شبعٌ في وِردِهِ الصدرُ

والناسُ قالوا هوَ المجنونُ ماذا عسى

يبغي من الحبِّ أو يرجو فيصطبرُ؟

أفي هوى تلك يستدمي محاجره

وليس في تلك ما يحلو ويعتبرُ!

فقلْ همُ البهمُ ماتوا قبلما وُلدوا

أنّى دروا كنهَ من يحيي وما اختبروا!

OF LOVE

Now should you meet a lover lost,
   Bewildered, yet avoiding guide,
Disdaining though he thirsts to drink,
   In his own hunger satisfied;

Hear people say, 'This youth bewitched
   'What seek he from a love so great?
'What hope has he to patiently
   'Await his Kismet and his Fate?

'Why waste his bloodstained tears for one
   'Who lacks all beauty and respect?'
Say of them all, they are stillborn,
   Know naught of life, nor can reflect.

ليس في الغابات عذلٌ

لا ولا فيها الرقيبْ

فاذا الغزلانُ جُنَّتْ

اذ ترى وجه المغيبْ

لا يقولُ النسرُ واهاً

ان ذا شيءٌ عجيبْ

انما العاقل يدعى

عندنا الامر الغريبْ

In the woods no blame attaches
   To lover's tryst, nor watchers spy;
When a gazelle, ranging swiftly,
   Greets its lovemate with a cry,

Eagles never display wonder,
   Or say, ''Tis marvel of the age.'
For in nature we the children
   Only hold the sane as strange.

إذا الشَّعْبُ يَوْماً أَرَادَ الحياة

فلا بُدَّ أنْ يَسْتَجيبَ القَدَرْ

وَلا بُدَّ للَّيْلِ أنْ يَنْجَلي

وَلا بُدَّ للقَيْدِ أنْ يَنْكَسِرْ

وَمَنْ لَمْ يُعانِقْهُ شَوْقُ الحَياة

تَبَخَّرَ في جَوِّها، وانْدَثَرْ

فَوَيْلٌ لِمَنْ لَمْ تَشُقْهُ الحيَاة

مِنْ صَفْعَةِ العدَم المُنْتَصِرْ

كذلِكَ قالَتْ لِيَ الكائنَات

وحَدَّثَني روحُها المُسْتَتِرْ

ودَمدَمَتِ الرّيحُ بين الفِجَاج

وَفَوْقَ الجِبالِ وتَحتَ الشَّجَرْ:

"إذا ما طَمَحْتُ إلى غايَةٍ

رَكِبْتُ المُنَى، ونَسِيتُ الحَذَرْ

ولَمْ أتَجَنَّبْ وُعُورَ الشِّعاب

ولا كُبَّةَ اللَّهَبِ المُسْتَعِرْ

ومَنْ لا يُحِبّ صُعُودَ الجِبال

يَعِشْ أبَدَ الدَّهرِ بين الحُفَرْ"

178

THE WILL OF LIFE

If one day the people should choose life
Fate is certain to respond.
The night will surely retreat,
and fetters be broken!
He who is not embraced by
    the longing for life
Will evaporate in vacancy
    and be forgotten –
Grief to anyone not aroused by
    the breathing desire for life!
Let him beware the slap of oblivion!
This is what life said to me,
this is how its spirit spoke.

The wind muttered between
    the ravines;
'When I aspire to a goal,
I ride my wishes, forgetting caution,
face the wilderness, the rugged trails
and flaming days –
He who does not like scaling mountains
will live eternally in potholes.'

So the sap of youth churned in my heart
as other winds raged within my breast.
I bent my head, listening to
the clap of thunder,

فَعَجَّتْ بِقَلْبِي دِماءُ الشَّباب
وَضَجَّتْ بِصَدْرِي رِياحٌ أُخَرْ...
وَأَطْرَقْتُ، أُصْغِي لِقَصْفِ الرُّعُود
وَعَزْفِ الرِّياحِ، وَوَقْعِ المَطَرْ

وَقالَتْ لِيَ الأَرْضُ ـ لَمَّا سَأَلت
"أَيا أُمُّ هَلْ تَكرَهِينَ البَشَرْ؟"
"أُبارِكُ في النَّاسِ أَهْلَ الطُّموح
وَمَنْ يَسْتَلِذُّ رُكُوبَ الخَطَرْ
وَأَلعَنُ مَنْ لا يُماشِي الزَّمانَ،
وَيَقْنَعُ بالعَيْشِ عَيْشَ الحَجَرْ
هُوَ الكَوْنُ حَيٌّ، يُحِبُّ الحَياة
وَيَحتَقِرُ المَيْتَ، مَهْما كَبُرْ
فَلا الأُفْقُ يَحضُنُ مَيْتَ الطُّيور،
وَلا النَّحلُ يَلثِمُ مَيْتَ الزَّهَرْ
وَلَوْلا أُمُومَةُ قَلْبِي الرَّؤوم
لَما ضَمَّتِ المَيْتَ تِلْكَ الحُفَرْ
فَوَيْلٌ لِمَنْ لَمْ تَشُقْهُ الحَياة،
مِنْ لَعْنَةِ العَدَمِ المُنتَصِرْ!"

وَفي لَيْلَةٍ مِنْ لَيالِي الخَريف
مُثَقَّلَةٍ بالأَسَى وَالضَّجَرْ

the chime of the draft,
the cadence of the rain.

When I asked the earth,
'Mother, do you hate mankind?'
She replied, 'I bless those
        with ambition,
those who brave danger –
I curse the ones not keeping
        step with time,
Who are content to live
        a fossil life.
The vibrating universe
        loves what moves
and despises the dead,
        forgetting their greatness.
The horizon hugs no
        stiffened bird
nor does the bee kiss
        a withered flower.
Not even graves would
        hold the dead,
save for the tenderness
        in my motherly heart!
Woe to one not longing
        for life!
Let him beware the curse
        of extinction!'

*

سَكِرْتُ بِهَا مِنْ ضِيَاء النجوم

وَغَنَّيْتُ للحُزْنِ حَتى سَكِرْ

سَألتُ الدُّجَى: هَل تُعِيدُ الحَياة

لِمَنْ أذْبَلَتْهُ رَبِيعَ العُمْرْ؟

فَلَمْ تَتَكَلَّمْ شِفاهُ الظَّلام

وَلَمْ تَتَرَنَّمْ عَذارَى السَّحَرْ

وَقالَ لِيَ الغابُ في رِقَّةٍ

مُحَبَّبَةٍ مِثلِ خَفْقِ الوَتَرْ:

"يَجيءُ الشِّتاءُ، شتاءُ الضَّباب،

شِتاءُ الثَّلوجِ، شتاء المَطَرْ

فَيَنْطَفِئُ السِّحرُ، سِحرُ الغُصُون،

وَسِحرُ الزُّهُور، وَسِحرُ الثَّمَرْ

وسِحرُ السّماءِ، الشَّجِيُّ، الوَديع،

وَسِحرُ المُرُوجِ، الشَّهِيُّ، العَطِرْ

وَتَهْوِي الغُصُونُ، وأوْرَاقُها

وأزْهَارُ عَهْدِ حَبِيبٍ نَضِرْ

وَتَلْهُو بِها الرِّيحُ في كُلِّ واد

وَيَدْفِنُها السَّيْلُ، أنّى عَبَرْ

وَيَفْنَى الجَمِيعُ، كَحُلْمٍ بَدِيع

تألَّقَ في مُهْجَةٍ وَانْدَثَرْ

وتَبْقَى البُذُورُ، التي حُمِّلَتْ

ذَخِيرَةَ عُمْرٍ جَمِيلٍ، غَبَرْ

On an autumn night
      laden with boredom,
I was so drunk on starlight
      my sadness drank too.
I asked the dark, 'Does life
      return the spring of youth
once it is withered?'
The lips of darkness did not move
nor did the virginal dawn.
Then the forest gently spoke
like the quiver of a chord:

      'Winter comes, winter of mist,
      winter of snow, winter of rain,
and magic dissolves.
What budded and ripened,
the gleaming angles of fields
and quiet magic of the sky –
gone like branches
that fall with their leaves.
Now the wind tosses dead petals,
the flood buries them haphazardly.
All perish like a lovely dream
Which shimmered in some heart
      then disappeared.
Only the seeds remain,
      kernels of memory,
still embracing, even under
      the fog, the snows,

وَذِكْرَى فُصُولٍ، ورُؤْيا حَياة،

وَأشباحَ دُنْيا، تَلاشَتْ زُمَرْ

مُعَانِقَةٌ ـ وَهيَ تَحتَ الضّبَاب،

وَتَحتَ الثُلُوج، وَتَحتَ المَدَرْ ـ

لِطَيْفِ الحيَاةِ الذي لا يُمَلّ

وَقَلْبُ الرّبيعِ الشّذِيِّ الخَضِرْ

وَحَالِمَةً بِأغَاني الطّيُور،

وَعِطْرِ الزّهُورِ، وَطَعْمِ الثّمَرْ

وَيَمشي الزّمانُ، فتَنمُو صُرُوف

وَتَذوِي صُرُوفٌ، وَتَحيا أُخَرْ

وَتُصبِحُ أحْلامُهَا يَقْظَةً،

مُوَشّحَةً بِغُمُوضِ السّحَرْ

تُسائِلُ: أينَ ضَبَابُ الصّبَاح؟

وَسحرُ المَسَاء؟ وَضَوْءُ القَمَرْ؟

وأسرابُ ذاكَ الفَرَاشِ الأنيق؟

وَنَحْلٌ يُغَنّي، وَغَيْمٌ يَمُرْ؟

وَأيْنَ الأشِعّةُ وَالكَائِنَات؟

وأينَ الحياةُ التي أنتَظِرْ؟

ظَمِئْتُ إلى النّورِ فَوْقَ الغُصُون!

ظَمِئْتُ إلى الظّلّ تحتَ الشّجَرْ!

the heaps of earth –
the shadow of life that never palls,
the green germ of spring
dreaming of birdcall,
the musk of flowers,
the tang of fruit.

'Time and trouble tumble on,
seasons wilt, others are reborn.
Dreams awaken laced with the mystery
of daybreak, asking,
    "Where is the morning mist?
The evening's magic? The glow of the moon?
The elegant throng of butterflies?
The humming bees? Where are the clouds
    that floated by,
the sunbeams and creatures,
    the life we seek?"
I have grown thirsty for the
    sheen of light on branches,
thirsty for the shade beneath the tree!

ظَمِئتُ إلى النَّبعِ، بَينَ المُروج،

يُغَنّي، ويَرقُصُ فوق الزَّهَرْ!

ظَمِئتُ إلى نَغماتِ الطُّيور،

وَهَمْسِ النَّسِيم، ولحنِ المَطَرْ!

ظَمِئتُ إلى الكَوْنِ! أينَ الوُجُود

وأنّى أرى العالَمَ المُنتَظَرْ؟

هُوَ الكَوْنُ، خَلفَ سُباتِ الجمود

وفي أُفُقِ اليقظاتِ الكُبَرْ

وما هو إلّا كخَفْقِ الجَناح

حتّى نَما شَوْقُها وَانتَصَرْ

فَصَدَّعَتِ الأرْض مِنْ فَوْقِها،

وأبصرَتِ الكَوْنَ عَذبَ الصّوَرْ

وجاءَ الرّبيعُ، بأنْغامِهِ،

وأحْلامِهِ، وَصِباهُ العَطِرْ

وَقَبَّلَها قُبَلاً في الشِّفاه،

تُعِيدُ الشَّبابَ الذي قَدْ غَبَرْ

وقالَ لَها: قَد مُنِحتِ الحياةَ،

وخُلّدْتِ في نَسْلِكِ المُدّخَرْ

وباركَكِ النّورُ، فاستَقْبِلي

شبابَ الحياةِ وَخِصْبَ العُمُرْ

Thirsty for the fountain that
      sings through blossoming fields,
      for the voices of birds,
      the whisper of breeze, the rain's
      melody –
I am thirsty for the universe,
searching for the long-awaited world!
Maybe it lies beyond the reaches of our sleep
and we must awaken to find it.

'Like a wing's slight flutter,
the seed's longing sprouted
till it cracked
the surface of the earth
and beheld a world
of exquisite images.
And spring returned with its
parcels of dreams,
its sweet-smelling freshness,
and kissed the lips
of all which had faded,
saying, "You have been granted life,
immortalized in your abundant seed.
The light has blessed you –
now receive it!

ومَنْ تَعْبُدُ النّورَ أَحْلامُهُ،

يُبارِكُهُ النّورُ أنّى ظَهَرْ

إلَيكِ الفَضاءَ، إليكِ الضّياءَ،

إلَيكِ الثّرى، الحالَم، المُزْدَهِرْ!

إليكِ الجَمالَ الذي لا يَبيدْ!

إليكِ الوجودَ، الرّحيبَ النّضِرْ!

فميدي ــ كما شِئتِ ــ فوق الحُقول

بِحُلوِ الثِّمارِ وَغَضِّ الزّهَرْ

وَناجي النّسيمَ، وَناجي الغُيُوم،

وَناجي النّجُومَ، وَناجي القَمَرْ

وَناجي الحياةَ وأشواقَها،

وَفِتنَةَ هذا الوجودِ الأغَرّ

وشَفّ الدُجى عَن جَمالٍ عَميق

يَشُبُّ الخيالَ، ويُذكي الفِكَرْ

ومُدّ عَلى الكَوْنِ سِحرٌ غَريب،

يُصَرّفُهُ ساحِرٌ مُقْتَدِرْ

وضاءتْ شُمُوعُ النّجومِ الوِضاء،

وَضَاعَ البَخُورُ، بَخورُ الزّهَرْ

ورَفْرَفَ رُوحٌ، غَريبُ الجَمال،

بأجنحةٍ مِنْ ضِياءِ القَمَرْ

Whoever worships the light in
        their dreams
will be blessed by light
        wherever it shines.
Onward! To radiant spaces,
        and the dreamy blooming earth!
For you, whatever is luminous!
For you, undying Beauty
The field and breeze and stars
        will be your home.
Commune with the moon
        and the stirring of life and its charm."

'The diaphanous night revealed a Beauty
that kindled the mind.
A strange magic was flung
        across the skies
as a giant wizard
        lit the glittering stars.
Incense drifted from flowers
        on the moon's quiet wings . . .

ورَنَّ نَشيدُ الحَياةِ المُقدَّس

في هَيكلٍ، حالمٍ، قَدْ سُحِرْ

وأُعلِنَ في الكوْنِ: أنَّ الطُّموح

لَهيبُ الحياةِ، وَرُوحُ الظَّفَرْ

إذا طَمَحَتْ للحياةِ النّفُوس

فَلا بُدَّ أنْ يَستجيبَ القَدَرْ! "

a holy hymn ringing out in a temple!
Across the universe it was proclaimed:
Endeavor is the flame of life,
the heart of victory.
If the spirit chooses life,
Fate is certain to respond!'

لَدَى سُرُرٍ لِأَوْلَادِي

أَبُثُّ ٱلْحُبَّ مُنْفَرِدَا

صَلَاةُ ٱللَّيْلِ مِنْ قَلْبِي

وَقَدْ نَامُوا كَمَا سَهِدَا

عَلَى نَظَرَاتٍ مَفْتُونٍ

تُقَبِّلُهُمْ فَمًا وَيَدَا

تُتَابِعُ حُلْوَ أَنْفَاسٍ

وَتُحْصِيهَا لَهُمْ عَدَدَا

وَأَرْكَعُ شِبْهَ مُبْتَهِلٍ

وَلَمْ أَكُ دَاعِيًا أَحَدَا

كَأَنِّي ٱللَّيْلَ عَابِدُهُمْ

فَحَالِي حَالُ مَنْ عَبَدَا

أَرَى ٱلْإِيمَانَ يَغْمُرُنِي

فَلَسْتُ بِمُسْرِفٍ أَبَدَا

وَلَكِنِّي أَبٌ حَانٍ

أَحَبَّ ٱللهَ وَٱلْوَلَدَا

وَقَدْ جُمِعَا بِنَظْرَتِهِ

وَفِي أَحْلَامِهَا خَلَدَا

EVENING PRAYER

Near the couch my children lie
Whispering my love am I,
Lonely at my wakeful prayer
While they sleep serenely there.
Little hand and mouth I kiss
With my gaze of raptured bliss,
Counting over for love's sake
Every precious breath they take.
As a suppliant I kneel
(Though none heedeth my appeal),
Venerating them this night
Like the truest anchorite;
Faith, methinks, o'erwhelms my soul,
That was never prodigal.
With a father's love I yearn,
To my son, and God, I turn;
In one gaze I capture them,
Bliss eternal in a dream.

AHMAD ZAKI ABU SHADI
TRANS. A. J. ARBERRY

وجدتُها في يوم صحوٍ جميل
وجدتُها بعد ضياع طويل
جديدة التربة مُخْضَوْضِره
نديانة مزهره
وجدتُها والشَّمس عبر النّخيل
تنثر في الحدائق المعشبه
باقاتها المذهبه
وكان نيسان السخيّ المريع
والحبِّ والدّفء وشمس الرّبيع

وجدتُها بعد ضياع طويل
غصناً طرياً دائم الاخضرار
تأوي له الاطيار
فيحتويها في حماه الظّليل
ان عبرت يوماً به عاصفه
راعدة من حوله راجفه
مال خفيفاً تحتها وانحنى
امامها ليِّنا
وتهدأ الزّوبعة القاصفه
ويستوي الغصن كما كانا

I FOUND IT

I found it on a radiant day
after a long drifting.
It was green and blossoming
as the sun over palm trees
scattered golden bouquets;
April was generous that season
with loving and sun.

I found it
after a long wandering.
It was a tender evergreen bough
where birds took shelter,
a bough bending gently under storms
which later was straight again,

مُشَعْشع الأوراق ريّانا
لم تنحطم أعطافه اللّدنه
تحت يد الرّيح
ويمضي كما
كان، كأن لم تثنه محنه
يضاحك الجمال في كل ما
يراه، في اشراقة النّجمه
في هفّة النّسمه
في الشّمس في الانداء في الغيمه

وجدتُها في يوم صحو جميل
بعد ضياع بعد بحث طويل
بُحَيْرة رائقة ساجيه
ان ولغت مرّه
في قلبها الصّافي ذئاب البشر
او عبثت فيها رياح القدر
تعكّرت فتره
ثم صفت صفاء بلّلورِ
ورجعت مرآة وجه القمر
ومسبح الزرقة والنور
ومستحمّ الانجم الهادية

rich with sap,
never snapping in the wind's hand.
It stayed supple
as if there were no bad weather,
echoing the brightness of stars,
the gentle breeze,
the dew and the clouds.

I found it
on a vivid summer day
after a long straying,
a tedious search.
It was a quiet lake
where thirsty human wolves
and swirling winds could only briefly
disturb the waters.
Then they would clear again like crystal
to be the moon's mirror,
swimming place of light and blue,
bathing pool for the guardian stars.

وجدتُها، يا عاصفات اعصفي

وقنِّعي بالسحب وجه السما

ما شئت، يا ايّام دوري كما

قُدّر لي، مشمسةً ضاحكه

أو جهمة حالكه

فان انواريَ لا تنطفي

وكلُّ ما قد كان من ظلِّ

يمتدّ مسوداً على عمري

يلفَّه ليلاً على ليلِ

مضى، ثوى في هوّة الامس

يوم اهتدت نفسي الى نفسي

I found it!
And now when the storms wail
and the face of the sun is masked in clouds,
when my shining fate revolves to dark,
my light will never be extinguished!
Everything that shadowed my life
wrapping it with night after night
has disappeared, lain down
in memory's grave,
since the day
my soul found
my soul.

FADWA TUQAN   199
TRANS. PATRICIA ALANAH BYRNE,
SALMA JAYYUSI AND NAOMI SHIHAB NYE

عيناكِ غابتا نخيلٍ ساعةَ السحَرْ،
أو شُرفتان راح ينأى عنهما القمر.
عيناك حين تبسمان تورق الكرومْ
وترقص الأضواء ... كالأقمار في نهَرْ
يرجّه المجذاف وهْناً ساعة السَّحر
كأنّما تنبض في غوريهما، النّجومْ ...

وتغرقان في ضبابٍ من أسىً شفيفْ
كالبحر سرَّح اليدين فوقه المساء،
دفء الشتاء فيه وارتعاشة الخريف،
والموت، والميلاد، والظلام، والضياء؛
فتستفيق ملء روحي، رعشة البكاء
ونشوةٌ وحشيّةٌ تعانق السماء
كنشوة الطفل إذا خاف من القمر!
كأن أقواس السحاب تشرب الغيومْ
وقطرةً فقطرةً تذوب في المطر...
وكركر الأطفالُ في عرائش الكروم،
ودغدغت صمت العصافير على الشجر
أنشودةُ المطر...
مطر...

RAIN SONG

Your eyes are two palm tree forests in early light,
Or two balconies from which the moonlight recedes
When they smile, your eyes, the vines put forth their leaves,
And lights dance . . . like moons in a river
Rippled by the blade of an oar at break of day;
As if stars were throbbing in the depths of them . . .

And they drown in a mist of sorrow translucent
Like the sea stroked by the hand of nightfall;
The warmth of winter is in it, the shudder of autumn,
And death and birth, darkness and light;
A sobbing flares up to tremble in my soul
And a savage elation embracing the sky,
Frenzy of a child frightened by the moon.
It is as if archways of mist drank the clouds
And drop by drop dissolved in the rain . . .
As if children snickered in the vineyard bowers,
The song of the rain
Rippled the silence of birds in the trees . . .
Drop, drop, the rain . . .
Drip . . .
Drop . . . the rain . . .

مطر...

مطر...

تثاءب المساء، والغيومُ ما تزالْ

تسحُّ ما تسحّ من دموعها الثقالْ.

كأنَّ طفلاً بات يهذي قبل أن ينام:

بأنَّ أُمَّه ــ التي أفاق منذ عامْ

فلم يجدها، ثمَّ حين لجَّ في السؤال

قالوا له: "بعد غدٍ تعودْ .." ــ

لا بدَّ أن تعودْ

وإنْ تهامس الرفاق أنَّها هناكْ

في جانب التلِّ تنام نومة اللّحودْ

تسفُّ من ترابها وتشرب المطر؛

كأن صياداً حزيناً يجمع الشِّباك

ويلعن المياه والقَدَر

وينثر الغناء حيث يأفل القمرْ.

مطر..

مطر..

أتعلمين أيَّ حُزْنٍ يبعث المطر؟

وكيف تنشج المزاريب إذا انهمر؟

وكيف يشعر الوحيد فيه بالضّياع؟

بلا انتهاء ــ كالدَّم المراق، كالجياع،

كالحبِّ، كالأطفال، كالموتى ــ هو المطر !

Evening yawned, from low clouds
Heavy tears are streaming still.
It is as if a child before sleep were rambling on
About his mother (a year ago he went to wake her, did not
    find her,
Then was told, for he kept on asking,
'After tomorrow, she'll come back again . . .')
That she must come back again,
Yet his playmates whisper that she is there
In the hillside, sleeping her death for ever,
Eating the earth around her, drinking the rain;
As if a forlorn fisherman gathering nets
Cursed the waters and fate
And scattered a song at moonset,
Drip, drop, the rain . . .
Drip, drop, the rain . . .

Do you know what sorrow the rain can inspire?.
Do you know how gutters weep when it pours down?
Do you know how lost a solitary person feels in the rain?
Endless, like spilt blood, like hungry people, like love,
Like children, like the dead, endless the rain.

ومقلتاك بي تطيفان مع المطر
وعبر أمواج الخليج تمسح البروقْ
سواحلَ العراق بالنجوم والمحار،
كأنها تهمّ بالشروق
فيسحب الليل عليها من دم دثارْ.
أصيح بالخليج: "يا خليجْ
يا واهب اللؤلؤ، والمحار، والرّدى!"
فيرجعُ الصَدى
كأنّه النشيجْ:
" يا خليج
يا واهب المحار والردى .."

أكاد أسمع العراق يذْخرُ الرعودْ
ويخزن البروق في السّهول والجبالْ،
حتى إذا ما فضَّ عنها ختمها لرّجالْ
لم تترك الرياح من ثمودْ
في الوادِ من أثرْ
أكاد أسمع النخيل يشربُ المطر
وأسمع القرى تئنّ، والمهاجرين
يصارعون بالمجاذيف وبالقلوع،
عواصف الخليج، والرعود، منشدين:
" مطر ...

Your two eyes take me wandering with the rain,
Lightnings from across the Gulf sweep the shores of Iraq
With stars and shells,
As if a dawn were about to break from them,
But night pulls over them a coverlet of blood.
I cry out to the Gulf: 'O Gulf,
Giver of pearls, shells and death!'
And the echo replies,
As if lamenting:
'O Gulf,
Giver of shells and death . . .'

I can almost hear Iraq husbanding the thunder,
Storing lightning in the mountains and plains,
So that if the seal were broken by men
The winds would leave in the valley not a trace of Thamud.
I can almost hear the palmtrees drinking the rain,
Hear the villages moaning and emigrants
With oar and sail fighting the Gulf
Winds of storm and thunder, singing
'Rain . . . rain . . .
Drip, drop, the rain . . .'

مطر ...

مطر ...

وفي العراق جوعْ

وينثر الغلالَ فيه موسم الحصادْ

لتشبع الغربان والجراد

وتطحن الشِّوان والحجر

رحىً تدور في الحقول ... حولها بشرْ

مطر ...

مطر...

مطر...

وكم ذرفنا ليلة الرحيل، من دموعْ

ثمَّ اعتللنا ـ خوف أن نلامَ ـ بالمطر...

مطر...

مطر...

ومنذ أنْ كنّا صغاراً، كانت السماء

تغيمُ في الشتاء

ويهطل المطر،

وكلَّ عام ـ حين يعشب الثرى ـ نجوعْ

ما مرَّ عامٌ والعراق ليس فيه جوعْ.

مطر...

مطر...

مطر...

And there is hunger in Iraq,
The harvest time scatters the grain in it,
That crows and locusts may gobble their fill,
Granaries and stones grind on and on,
Mills turn in the fields, with them men turning . . .
Drip, drop, the rain . . .
Drip . . .
Drop . . .

When came the night for leaving, how many tears we shed,
We made the rain a pretext, not wishing to be blamed
Drip, drop, the rain . . .
Drip, drop, the rain . . .
Since we had been children, the sky
Would be clouded in wintertime,
And down would pour the rain,
And every year when earth turned green the hunger
    struck us.
Not a year has passed without hunger in Iraq.
Rain . . .
Drip, drop, the rain . . .
Drip, drop . . .

في كل قطرة من المطر
حمراءُ أو صفراء من أجنَّة الزَّهَرْ.
وكلَّ دمعةٍ من الجياع والعراة
وكلَّ قطرة تراق من دم العبيدْ
فهي ابتسامٌ في انتظار مبسم جديد
أو حُلمةٌ توردَّتْ على فم الوليدْ
في عالم الغد الفتيّ، واهب الحياة!
مطر...
مطر...
مطر...
سيُعشبُ العراق بالمطر..."

أصيح بالخليج: "يا خليج..
يا واهب اللؤلؤِ، والمحار، والردى!"
فيرجع الصدى
كأنَّه النشيج:
"يا خليج
يا واهب المحار والردى."
وينثر الخليج من هِباته الكثارْ،
على الرمال، : رغوه الأُجاجَ، والمحار
وما تبقَّى من عظام بائسٍ غريق
من المهاجرين ظلَّ يشرب الردى

In every drop of rain
A red or yellow color buds from the seeds of flowers,
Every tear wept by the hungry and naked people,
Every spilt drop of slaves' blood,
Is a smile aimed at a new dawn,
A nipple turning rosy in an infant's lips,
In the young world of tomorrow, bringer of life.
Drip, drop, the rain . . .
Drip . . .
Drop . . . the rain . . .
Iraq will blossom one day in the rain.

I cry out to the Gulf: 'O Gulf,
Giver of pearls, shells and death!'
The echo replies
As if lamenting:
'O Gulf,
Giver of shells and death.'
And across the sands from among its lavish gifts
The Gulf scatters fuming froth and shells
And the skeletons of miserable drowned emigrants
Who drank death forever

من لجَّة الخليج والقرار،
وفي العراق ألف أفعى تشرب الرَّحيقْ
من زهرة يربُّها الفرات بالنَّدى.
وأسمع الصدى
يرنُّ في الخليج
"مطر...
مطر...
مطر...
في كلِّ قطرة من المطرْ
حمراء أو صفراء من أجنَّةِ الزَّهَرْ.
وكلِّ دمعة من الجياع والعراة
وكلِّ قطرةٍ تراق من دم العبيدْ
فهي ابتسامٌ في انتظار مبسم جديد
أو حُلمةٌ تورَّدت على فم الوليدْ
في عالم الغد الفتيّ، واهب الحياة."

ويهطُل المطرْ..

From the depths of the Gulf, from the ground of its silence,
And in Iraq a thousand serpents drink the nectar
From a flower the Euphrates has nourished with dew.
I hear the echo
Ringing in the Gulf:
'Rain . . .
Drip, drop, the rain . . .
Drip, drop.'
In every drop of rain
A red or yellow color buds from the seeds of flowers.
Every tear wept by the hungry and naked people
And every spilt drop of slaves' blood
Is a smile aimed at a new dawn,
A nipple turning rosy in an infant's lips
In the young world of tomorrow, bringer of life.

And still the rain pours down.

BADR SHAKIR AL-SAYYAB   211
TRANS. LENA JAYYUSI AND
CHRISTOPHER MIDDLETON

عصيرُ الزنبق الاسودِ في العينين والشعرِ
وشمسُ الهند قد تركتْ على الخدَّينْ
ألوفَ القبل الولهى، ومست رجفة الشفَتَين
بأحرق ما يصب الشوقُ في غمّازةِ الثغر.

غريباً مرَّ عن دنياي لن يحيى بماضيها
ولن يسري الى مستوطن الذكرى
مع الاحباب، بل يبقى نسيماً عابراً مرّا
على أزهارنا وأثاً حساً ناعماً فيها.

سيمضي، لن يراهُ الليلُ سهداً في مآقينا
ولن يشرب من آهاتنا حسرَهْ
ولا من دمعنا المغلوبِ في اعماقنا قطرَهْ
ولن يمتصُّ من اوراد خدَّينا التلاوينا.

ولن ينضمَّ في أغوارنا الولهى مع الاشجانْ،
فنُمضي بعده الايامَ ساعاتٍ بلا هدَفِ
ونعصرُ قلبنا المفجوع كي يرتاح من شغفِ
تهيمنَهُ، وكي يطويْهِ في دوّامة النسيانْ.

SHUDAN

Black lily's blood stains his eyes and hair,
on his cheeks India's sun burns a thousand ebony kisses,
burnishing his trembling, half-opened lips
with light approaching passion's intensest flame.

He entered my world, a stranger taking no part,
never stealing into my house of memory,
winning the honored place among my loves,
for like silk wind he but briefly caressed my flower.

He will go away and I won't lose any sleep over it,
he will not learn to drink regret from my sighs
or kiss away those tears I never shed for him,
plucking putative roses from my passionate cheeks.

He will not be numbered among my heart's cares
I won't waste my days in aimless hours on account of him
or squeeze my heart to give it rest, mad
to wrap him tight in the sweetness of oblivion.

سيمضي، لن يحطُّم وجه تاريخ ألفناهُ
ويقلق سرنا المدفون تحت تودد الاجفانْ
ويذعر زهرنا الملتاع من تَشرابنا الاحزانْ
فشودانُ، الفتى الشرقيُّ، عدَّى ما عرفناه.

أعن عبثٍ ترى شودان رفَّ على أمانينا
وغذَّى بالجمال الفذِّ اشواقاً تؤرِّقها
وروَّى الظمأ الخالد من حبٍ يشوّقها
الى الابداع، واستولى على احساسنا حِينا؛

أعن عبثٍ تُرى شودانُ لاح على هياكلنا
وذاق نشيدنا المرفوع تقديساً لمعبرِهِ
واطلق ضحكنا، وبخورنا النادر من وَقدات مجمرِهِ
ومرَّ، كما يمرّ الطيفُ، لم ينعُمْ بسقيا من مناهلنا

يحق لبحثنا الملهوف عن مجهولنا المُغري
وراء متاعبٍ نسعى اليها كي تمزِّقَنا
وراء أناملٍ تمتد تُغرينا وترهقنا
بأن يلقى هنيهةَ راحةٍ في لُجة العمرِ.

He will go away and not mar the still life I've chosen,
sleeping secrets in my eyes will not wake to madness,
he cannot further terrorize a heart already quelled by grief.
Shudan came and went, we never spoke a word.
Was it all for nothing he passed this way and by beauty
lit a beauty within that troubles me still, easing
love's deathless need for an instant so that I desire
to hurl myself at all that's pure and perfect in the world?

Was it all for nothing Shudan stopped before my
     temple gate
and heard the psalm I raise within, honoring his passing.
He made me laugh for joy while I burned incense to
     his name,
without offering in return one taste of nectar from my lips?

All in all it is good while we search for the unknown and fall,
gambling with perilous joys that rend body and soul,
lusting for the touch of hands that inflame, weary flesh,
to win from life a brief and timeless truce that cheats
     the grave.

سنا إشراقةٍ تهمي على آهاتنا الظمأى،
على احساسنا المترفِ في تَيهانه الذاتي
هنيهة فرحةٍ، إنا حَيينا بالهُنيهات
نوازفُ كأسنا كثر ولكن كأسنا ملأى.

It was good he paused before me, this sudden storm of light
stirring dead hope, clear spark of beauty uncut by pain.
These times give meaning to my life and make me whole:
my cup has many cracks yet the wine always kissed
   the brim.

SALMA KHADRA JAYYUSI
TRANS. CHARLES DORIA

أُريدُ أن أكتبَ لكِ كلاماً
لا يُشْبِهُ الكلامْ.
وأخترعَ لغةً لكِ وحْدَكِ
أُفَصِّلُها على مقاييس جَسَدِكِ
ومَسَاحةِ حُبّي.

أُريدُ أن أُسافرَ من أوراق القامُوسْ
وأطلبَ إجازةً من فمي.
فلقد تعبتُ من اسْتِدَارة فَمي
أُريدُ فَماً آخَرْ..
يستطيعُ أن يتحوَّلَ متى أراذْ
إلى شَجَرة كَرَزْ..
أو عُلْبة كبريتْ..
أُريدُ فماً جديداً تخرجُ منه الكلماتْ
كما تخرجُ الحوريَّاتُ من زَبَد البحرْ
وكما تخرجُ الصِّيصَانُ البيضاءُ من قُبَّعة السَّاحرْ..

I WANT TO WRITE DIFFERENT WORDS FOR YOU

I want to write different words for you
To invent a language for you alone
To fit the size of your body
And the size of my love.

I want to travel away from the dictionary
And to leave my lips
I am tired of my mouth
I want a different one
Which can change
Into a cherry tree or a match box,
A mouth from which words can emerge
Like nymphs from the sea,
Like white chicks jumping from the magician's hat.

NIZAR QABBANI   219
TRANS. BASSAM K. FRANGIEH AND
CLEMENTINA R. BROWN

خُذُوا جميعَ الكُتُب التي قرأتُها في طُفُولتي
خُذُوا جميعَ كَرَاريسي المدرسيّهْ
خُذُوا الطَبَاشيرَ.. والأقلامَ.. والألواحَ السوداءْ..
وعَلِّمُوني كلمةً جديدَهْ
أعلِّقُها كالحَلَقِ في أُذْن حبيبتي..

أريدُ أصابعَ أُخْرَى..
لأكتُبَ بطريقةٍ أُخْرَى..
فأنا أكرهُ الأصابعَ التي لا تطولُ.. ولا تقصُرْ.
كما أكرهُ الأشجارَ التي لا تموتُ.. ولا تكبُرْ.
أريدُ أصابعَ جَديدَةً..
عاليةً كصواري المراكبْ
وطويلةً كأعناق الزُرافَاتْ
حتى أفصِّلَ لحبيبتي قميصاً من الشِعْر..
لم تلِبسْهُ قَبْلي..

TAKE ALL THE BOOKS

Take all the books
That I read in my childhood,
Take all my school notebooks,
Take the chalk,
The pens,
And the blackboards,
But teach me a new word
To hang like an earring
On my lover's ear.

I want new fingers
To write in another way,
High like masts of ships,
Long like a giraffe's neck
So I can tailor for my beloved
A garment of poetry.

NIZAR QABBANI
TRANS. BASSAM K. FRANGIEH AND
CLEMENTINA R. BROWN

أريدُ أن أصنعَ لكِ أبْجَديَّةً
غيرَ كلِّ الأبْجَديَّاتْ.
فيها شيءٌ من إيقاع المَطَرْ..
وشيءٌ من غُبَار القَمَرْ..
وشيءٌ من حزن الغُيُوم الرماديَّة
وشيءٌ من تَوَجُّع أوراق الصَفْصَاف
تحتَ عَرَباتِ أيلولْ.

I WANT TO MAKE YOU A UNIQUE ALPHABET

I want to make you a unique alphabet
In it I want
The rhythm of the rain,
The dust of the moon,
The sadness of the grey clouds,
The pain of the fallen willow leaves
Under the wheels of autumn.

NIZAR QABBANI
TRANS. BASSAM K. FRANGIEH AND
CLEMENTINA R. BROWN

ماحياً كل حكمةٍ /
هذه ناريَ /
لم تبقَ آيةٌ ــ دميَ الآيةُ /
هذا بدئي /

دخلتُ إلى حوضكِ /
أرضٌ تدور حوليَ أعضاؤكِ نيلٌ يجري /
طفَوْنا ترسّبْنا / تقاطعتِ في دمي قطعَتْ صدركِ أمواجيَ
انهصرتِ لنبْدأ : نسيَ الحبُّ شفرَةَ الليلِ / هل أصرخُ
أنَّ الطوفان يأتي؟ / لنبْدأ: صرخةٌ تعرج المدينةَ والناسُ
مرايا تمشي / إذا عبَر الملحُ التقينا هل أنتِ؟ /

ــ حبّيَ جرحٌ
جسَدي وردةٌ على الجرح لا يُقطَفُ إلا موتاً. دمي
غُصُنٌ أسلم أوراقَه استقرَّ...

هل الصخرُ جوابٌ؟ هل موتكِ السيدُ النائم يُغْوي؟
عندي لثديك هالاتُ وَلوع لوجهك الطفل وجهٌ مثلهُ...
أنتِ؟ لم أجدكِ
وهذا لهبي ماحياً

From THIS IS MY NAME

Erasing every wisdom /
    This is my fire /
    No sign remained – My blood is the sign /
    This is my beginning /

I entered your enclosure /
    Earth revolving around me, your organs a Nile flowing /
We drifted, we settled / You intersected my blood and my
waves crossed your chest, you broke apart. Let us begin:
Love forgot the blade-edge of night / Shall I scream that the
flood is coming? / Let us begin: A scream scales the city and
the people are mirrors walking / When the salt has crossed,
we shall meet. Is it you?

– My love is a wound
    My body a rose upon the wound, unpluckable except at
death. My blood is a bough that surrendered its leaves and
then settled down . . .

    Is the stone an answer? Does your death, that sleeping
master, beguile you? I have halos of craving for your
breasts, for your child-like face a face like it . . . You? I did not
find you
    This is my flame which erases.

دخلت إلى حوضكِ عندي مدينةٌ تحت أحزانَي
عندي ما يجعل الغُصْنَ الاخضرَ افعى والشمسَ عاشقةً
سوداءَ عندي... /

تقدّموا فقراءَ الأرض غطّوا هذا الزّمان بأسمالٍ
ودمْع غطّوه بالجسد الباحث عن دفئه... المدينةُ
أقواسُ جُنونٍ / رأيتُ أن تلدَ الثورة أبناءها، قبرت
ملايين الأغاني وجئتُ (هل أنت في قبريَ)؟ هاتي ألمسْ
يديك اتبعيني زَمني لم يجئْ ومقبرة العالم جاءت / عندي
لكلّ السلاطين رمادٌ / هاتي يديك اتبعيني...

قادرٌ ان أغيّر: لغْمُ الحضارة ــ هذا هو اسمي
(لافتة)

I entered your enclosure. Beneath my sorrows, I have a city, I have what makes vipers of the green branches, of the sun a black lover, I have ... /

Approach, you wretched of the earth, cover this age in rags and tears, cover it with a body searching for its warmth ... The city is arcs of madness / I believed that the revolution bore its children. I buried millions of songs and I came. (Are you in my grave?) Come that I may touch your hands: Follow me. My time has not come but the graveyard of the world has / I have ashes for all the sultans / Give me your hands: Follow me ...

I am able to transform: the land-mine of civilization – this is my name
  (a sign)

ADONIS   227
TRANS. SHAWKAT M. TOORAWA

منذ أن خلق البرد والابواب المغلقة
وأنا أمدّ يدي كالأعمى
بحثاً عن جدار
أو امرأة تؤويني
ولكن ماذا تفعل الغزالة العمياء
بالنّبع الجاري؟
والبلبل الأسير
بالأفق الذي يلامس قضبانه؟
في عصر الذّرة والعقول الالكترونية
في زمن العطر والغناء والأضواء الخافتة
كنت أحدثها عن حداء البدو
والسّفر إلى الصّحراء
على ظهور الجمال
ونهداها يصغيان إليّ
كما يصغي الأطفال الصّغار
لحديث ممتع حول الموقد
كنّا نحلم بالصّحراء
كما يحلم الرّاهب بالمضاجعة
واليتيم بالمزمار
وكنت أقول لها وأنا أرسل

DREAM

Since cold and closed doors were created,
I, like the blind, have stretched out my hands,
Searching for a wall
Or a woman to shelter me.
But what can the blind gazelle do with a flowering spring?
The captive nightingale with the horizon which brushes the
  bars of his cage?

In the age of the atom and the electronic brain,
In the time of perfume, soft light and song,
I told her of Bedouin chanting,
Of journeying to the desert
On camelback,
And her young breasts listened to me,
As little children sitting around a fire
Listen to a charming tale.
We were dreaming of the desert
As the monk dreams of a woman's arms,
And the orphan, of a flute.

I said to her, as I cast my gaze
On the distant horizon:
There on the blue sands we will lie
And sleep silently till daybreak,
Not for want of words,
But because the weary butterflies

نظراتي إلى الأفق البعيد:
هناك نتّكئ على الرّمال الزّرقاء
وننام صامتين حتى الصّباح
لا لأنّ الكلمات قليلة
ولكن لأنّ الفراشات المتعبة
تنام على شفاهنا.
غداً يا حبيبتي غدا
نستيقظ مبكرين
مع الملاحين وأشرعة البحر
ونرتفع مع الرّيح كالطّيور
كالدّماء عند الغضب
ونهوي على الصّحراء
كما يهوي الفم على الفم
ونمنا متعانقين طوال اللّيل
وأيدينا على حقائبنا
وفي الصّباح أقلعنا عن السّفر
لأنّ الصّحراء كانت في قلبينا.

Will be sleeping on our lips.
Tomorrow, o beloved, tomorrow
We will awaken early with the sailors and their sails,
And we will rise on the wind
Like birds,
Like raging blood,
And roam over the desert
As lips roam over lips.
Locked in embrace, we slept throughout the night,
Our hands upon our baggage.
And in the morning
We renounced our journey
For the desert was in our hearts.

MUHAMMAD AL-MAGHUT   231
TRANS. MOUNAH A. KHOURI AND HAMID ALGAR

لِنَذْهَبْ كما نَحْنُ:

سيِّدةً حُرَّةً

وصديقاً وفيّاً،

لنذهبْ معاً في طريقَيْنِ مُخْتَلِفَين

لنذهبْ كما نحنُ مُتَّحِدَيْن

ومُنْفَصِلَيْن،

ولا شيءَ يُوجِعُنا

لا طلاقُ الحمام ولا البردُ بين اليَدَيْن

ولا الريحُ حول الكنيسة تُوجِعُنا...

لم يكن كافياً ما تفتَّح من شَجَر اللوز

فابتسمي يُزْهر اللوزُ أكثر

بين فراشات غمازَتَيْن.

وعمّا قليلٍ يكونُ لنا حاضرٌ آخَرٌ

إن نَظَرْتِ وراءك لن تبصري

غيرَ منفى وراءك:

غُرْفَةُ نومِكِ،

صفصافةُ الساحةِ،

النهرُ خلف مباني الزجاج،

ومقهى مواعيدنا... كُلُّها، كُلّها

WE WERE MISSING A PRESENT

Let's go as we are:
a free woman
and a loyal friend,
let's go together on two different paths
let's go as we are united
and separate,
with nothing hurting us
not the divorce of the doves or the coldness between
    the hands
nor the wind around the church . . .
what bloomed of almond trees wasn't enough.
So smile for the almonds to blossom more
between the butterflies of two dimples

And soon there will be a new present for us.
If you look back you will see only
the exile of your looking back:
your bedroom,
the courtyard willow,
the river behind the glass buildings,
and the café of our trysts . . . all of it, all

تَسْتَعِدُّ لتصبح منفيٍّ، إذاً
فلنكن طيّبين!

لِنَذْهَبْ كما نَحْنُ:
إنسانةً حُرّةً
وصديقاً وفيّاً لناياتها،
لم يكن عُمْرُنا كافياً لنشيخ معاً
ونسيرَ إلى السينما متعبين
ونَشْهَدَ خاتمةَ الحرب بين أثينا وجاراتها
ونرى حفلة السلم ما بين روما وقرطاج
عمّا قليل.
فعمّا قليلٍ ستنتقل الطَيْرُ من زَمَنٍ نحو آخَرَ،
هل كان هذا الطريقُ هباءً
على شَكْلِ معنى، وسار بنا
سَفَراً عابراً بين أسطورتين
فلا بُدَّ منه، ولا بُدَّ منا
غريباً يرى نَفْسَهُ في مرايا غريبته؟
"لا، ليس هذا طريقي إلى جَسَدي
"لا حُلولَ ثقافيّةً لهُمُومٍ وُجوديّة
"أينما كنتَ كانت سمائي
حَقيقيّة
"مَنْ أنا لأُعيد لَكَ الشمسَ والقَمَرَ السابقين
فلنكن طيّبين...

234

preparing to become exile, so
let's be kind!

Let's go as we are:
a free woman
and a friend loyal to her flutes.
Our time wasn't enough to grow old together
to walk wearily to the cinema
to witness the end of Athens's war with her neighbors
and see the banquet of peace between Rome and Carthage
about to happen. Because soon
the birds will relocate from one epoch to another:
Was this path only dust
in the shape of meaning, and did it march us
as if we were a passing journey between two myths
so the path is inevitable, and we are inevitable
as a stranger sees himself in the mirror of another stranger?
'No, this is not my path to my body'
'No cultural solutions for existential concerns'
'Wherever you are my sky
is real'
'Who am I to give you back the previous sun and moon'
Then let's be kind . . .

لنذهبْ، كما نحن:
عاشقةً حُرَّةً
وشاعرَها.
لم يكن كافياً ما تساقط من
ثلج كانون أوَّل، فابتسمي
يندف الثلج قطناً على صلوات المسيحيّ،
عمَّا قليلٍ نعود إلى غَدِنا، خَلْفَنا،
حَيْثُ كُنَّا هناك صغيرين في أوَّل الحب،
نلعب قصة روميو وجولييت
كي نتعلَّم مُعْجَمَ شكسبير...
طار الفَرَاشُ مِنَ النَّوْم
مثل سرابِ سلام سريع
يُكَلِّلُنا نجمتين
ويقتلُنا في الصراع على الاسم
ما بين نافذتين
لنذهب، إذاً
ولنكن طيِّبين

لنَذْهَبْ، كما نَحْنُ:
إنسانةٌ حُرَّة
وصديقاً وفيّاً،
لنذهَبْ كما نحن. جئنا

Let's go, as we are:
a free lover
and her poet.
What fell of January snow
wasn't enough, so smile
for snow to card its cotton on the Christian's prayer,
we will soon return to our tomorrow, behind us,
where we were young in love's beginning,
playing Romeo and Juliet
and learning Shakespeare's language . . .
The butterflies have flown out of sleep
as a mirage of a swift peace
that adorns us with two stars
and kills us in the struggle over the name
between two windows
so, let's go
and let's be kind

Let's go, as we are:
a free woman
and a loyal friend,
let's go as we are. We came
with the wind from Babylon
and we march to Babylon . . .

مَعَ الريح من بابلٍ
ونسيرُ إلى بابلٍ...
لم يَكُنْ سَفَري كافياً
ليصير الصنَوْبَرُ في أَثَري
لفظةً لمديح المكان الجنوبيِّ
نحن هنا طَيِّبونَ. شَماليَّةٌ
ريحُنا، والأغاني جَنُوبيَّةٌ
هل أنا أنتِ أُخرى
وأنتِ أنا آخر؟
"ليس هذا طريقي إلى أرض حُرِّيَّتي
ليس هذا طريقي إلى جَسَدي
وأنا، لن أكون "أنا" مَرَّتين
وقد حَلَّ أمسِ مَحَلَّ غدي
وانقَسَمْتُ إلى امرأتين
فلا أنا شرقيَّةٌ
ولا أنا غربيَّةٌ،
ولا أنا زيتونةٌ ظَلَّلَتْ آيَتَين
لِتَذْهَبْ، إذاً،
"لا حلولَ جماعيَّةً لهواجسَ شخصيَّة
لم يكن كافياً أن نكون معاً
لنكون معاً...
كان ينقُصُنا حاضرٌ لنرى

My travel wasn't enough
for the pines to become in my trace
an utterance of praise to the southern place.
We are kind here. Northerly
is our wind, and our songs are southerly.
Am I another you
and you another I?
'This isn't my path to my freedom's land'
this isn't my path to my body
and I won't be 'I' twice
now that my yesterday has become my tomorrow
and I have split into two women
so I am not of the east
and I am not of the west,
nor am I an olive tree shading two verses in the Quran,
then let's go.
'No collective solutions for personal scruples'
it wasn't enough that we be together
to be together . . .
we were missing a present to see
where we were. Let's go as we are,

أَين نحن. لنذْهَبْ كما نحن،

إنسانةً حُرَّةً

وصديقاً قديماً

لنذهبْ معاً في طريقين مختلفين

لنذهب معاً،

ولنكن طيّبين...

a free woman
and an old friend
let's go on two separate paths
let's go together,
and let's be kind . . .

MAHMOUD DARWISH

TRANS. FADY JOUDAH

بكأس الشراب المرصّع باللازوردِ
انتظرها،
على بركة الماء حول المساء وزَهْر الكولُونيا
انتظرها،
بصبر الحصان المُعَدّ لِمُنْحَدرات الجبالِ
انتظرها،
بذَوْقِ الأمير الرفيع البديع
انتظرها،
بسبعِ وسائدَ مَحْشُوّةٍ بالسحابِ الخفيفِ
انتظرها،
بنار البَخُور النسائيّ ملءَ المكانِ
انتظرها،
برائحة الصَنْدَلِ الذَكَريّةِ حول ظُهور الخيولِ
انتظرها،
ولا تتعجَّلْ، فإن أقبلَتْ بعد موعدها
فانتظرها،
وإن أقبلتْ قبل موعدها
فانتظرها،
ولا تُجْفِل الطيرَ فوق جدائلها

A LESSON FROM KAMA SUTRA

With the drinking glass studded with lapis
wait for her,
by the pool around the evening and the rose perfume
wait for her,
with the patience of the horse prepared for mountain
    descent
wait for her,
with the manners of the refined and marvelous prince
wait for her,
with seven pillows stuffed with light clouds
wait for her,
with burning womanly incense filling up the place
wait for her,
with the sandalwood male scent around the backs of horses
wait for her,
and don't hurry, so if she arrives late
wait for her,
and if she arrives early
wait for her,
and don't startle the birds in her braids

وانتظرها،

لتجلس مرتاحةً كالحديقة في أَوْج زِينَتِها

وانتظرها،

لكي تتنفَّسَ هذا الهواء الغريبَ على قلبها

وانتظرها،

لترفع عن ساقها ثَوْبَها غيمةً غيمةً

وانتظرها،

وخُذْها إلى شرفة لترى قمراً غارقاً في الحليبِ

انتظرها،

وقدِّمْ لها الماءَ، قبل النبيذِ، ولا

تتطلَّعْ إلى تَوْأَمَيْ حَجَلٍ نامَّين على صدرها

وانتظرها،

ومُسَّ على مَهل يَدَها عندما

تَضَعُ الكأسَ فوق الرخام

كأنَّك تحملُ عنها الندى

وانتظرها،

تحدَّثْ إليها كما يتحدَّثُ نايٌ

إلى وَتَرٍ خائفٍ في الكمانِ

كأنكما شاهدانِ على ما يُعِدُّ غَدٌ لكما

وانتظرها،

and wait for her,
so that she sits comfortably in her beauty's summit in
    the garden
and wait for her,
so she may breathe this strange air upon her heart
and wait for her,
so that she lifts her dress off her calf cloud by cloud
and wait for her,
take her to a balcony to see a moon drowning in milk
and wait for her,
offer her water, before wine, and don't
look at twin partridges sleeping on her chest
and wait for her,
slowly touch her hand
when she places the glass on the marble
as if you were carrying dew for her
and wait for her,
talk to her as a flute talks
to a frightened violin string
as if you two were witnesses to what tomorrow prepares
    for you

ولَمِّع لها لَيْلَها خاتماً خاتماً
وانتظرها،
إلى أن يقولَ لَكَ الليلُ:
لم يَبْقَ غيركُما في الوجودِ
فخُذْها، بِرِفْقٍ، إلى موتكَ المُشْتَهى
وانتظرها!...

and wait for her
brighten her night ring by ring
and wait for her
until the night says to you:
You are the only two left in the universe
so take her, gently, to your desired death
and wait for her! . . .

MAHMOUD DARWISH
TRANS. FADY JOUDAH

١

تَشَظَّى أمْكِنَةٌ
وَهَوَاءُ
الصّبْحِ يَهُبُّ عَلَيَّ مِنَ الْغَلَسِ

٢

كَتِفِي لَمْ تَسْتَيْقِظْ بَعْدُ
إنَّهَا غَيْمَةٌ تَنْحَنِي
لِالْتِمَاعِ الْأَبْدِ

٣

هَلْ تَخْتَرِعُ الْأَشْجَارُ صَدَاهَا
أمْ
وَضَعَ الْأَعْمَى
يَدَهُ
فِي الْمَاءْ

ROSE OF DUST

1
Shattered places
and the breeze
of dawn wakes up on me

2
My shoulder still in slumber
Λ cloud bowing
to the flicker of infinity

3
Is it that trees invent their echo
or
has the blind
just dipped his hand
in water

٤

يُطْبِقُ الشَّاعِرُ
جَفْنَيْهِ
عَلَى وَرْدَةٍ
مِنْ غُبَارْ

٥

ذَبْذَبَاتٌ تَخْدِشُ نَافِذَتِي
أَغْصَانُ صَنَوْبَرَةٍ
تَهْتَزُّ قَلِيلاً
بَيْنَ رَمَادِ الثُّلُوجْ

٦

مَاءٌ أَمْلَسُ
مِنْ أَيِّ شُعُوبْ
عَادَتْ
رِيحٌ وَرَمَتْ بِزَبَرْجَدةٍ فِي الْمَاءْ

٧

مُمْكِنٌ لِلْعُزْلَةِ
أَنْ
تُفْضِي بِاسْتِئْنَافِ الْمُنْعَرَجَاتْ

4
The poet closes
his eyes
on a rose
of
dust

5
Scratching my window-pane
the pine tree
lightly shudders
under a snow of ashes

6
Smooth water
From which paleness
did the wind return
and throw another topaz in the river

7
Solitude
could
end with winding paths

بِالسَّكْرَة
بِالشَّطَحَاتْ
لَكِنْ كُلَّمَا حَاوَلْتُ سُؤالاً عَنْ مَعْنَى الْمَوْتْ
أبْصَرْتُ أَمَامِي سَيِّدَةً نَازِقَةً
خَرْسَاءْ

٨
اللَّيْلُ هُنَا يَعْوِي
طَرَقَاتٌ فِي جِهَةٍ مَا
وَأَنَا
أشْرَبُ مِنْ خَمْرَةِ هُلْدِرْلِين

٩
لَمْعَةٌ
لَمْعَتَانِ
هَذَا يَكْفِي لِلسَّاحِرِ
كَيْ
يَتَأَكَّدُ أَنَّ الْوَقْتَ أليفٌ
والشِّعْرَ نِدَاءْ

intoxication
trips
But whenever I inquire about death
a lady stands against me
impetuous and mute

8
The night barks here
Thumps somewhere
And I am drinking
Hölderlin's wine

9
A shimmer
Then another
Enough for the magician
to make sure
that time is tame
that poetry is a call

١٠

لَمْ يُبْصِرْنِي أَحَدٌ
وَأَنَا بِهُدُوءٍ أَفْتَحُ جَارُوراً
لأَرَى
أَيْنَ انْدَسَّتْ نَفْسِي

١١

لِعِظَامِي بَرْدٌ يقْضُمُهَا
هَلْ ثَمَّةَ إِسْمٌ
يَنْطَفِئُ اللَّيْلَةَ قَبْلِي

١٢

أَلْغَمَامُ الْغَمَامْ
رِقَّةٌ
قَفَزَتْ
كِدْتُ أَحْسَبُ أَنَّ يَدِي
مِنْ غَمَامْ

10
No one saw me
quietly opening a drawer
to see
where did my self
sneak in

11
My bones have their own biting frost
Is there a name that will go out
before me tonight

12
Clouds upon clouds
flutter
A leap
I almost thought my hand
was made of clouds

١٣

إلْعَبْ بِذُؤَابَةِ شِعْرِيَ

قُلْتُ أَنَا

فَانُوسٌ

زَرْبِيةٌ

ثَلْجٌ

وَجِدَارْ

١٤

خَطَفَتْ نَجْمَتَانِ يَدِي

لَحْظَةً

كُنْتُ أَرْمُقُهَا

ارْتَعَشَتْ

وَبَكَتْ

هَلْ أَنَا

أَمْ

أَنَا

13
Play with my poetry's lock
I say
I'm a lantern
a rug
a snow
a wall

14
Two stars kidnapped my hand
For a second
I watched it
tremble
weep
Am I
or am I

MOHAMMED BENNIS
TRANS. ANTON SHAMMAS

ينام في الغرفة المجاورة، بيننا جدار
ولا أقصد بهذا أيّ رموز مُحتملة
فقط... بيننا جدارٌ، أستطيعُ مَلأه بصور حبيبي، وهو
يدخن... أو يتأمّل
شرطَ أن أجدَ لها مكاناً محايداً
احتراماً للمسافة التي بيننا.

يبدو أن الله لا يحبني
كبُرتُ بما يكفي لأصدّق: الله لا يحبني من قديم، مُنذ
كان يحب أستاذَ الحساب، ويمنحه بصراً حاداً،
وطباشيرَ ملوّنةً
وفرصاً كثيرةً لتعذيب طفلةٍ مثلي
لا تستطيع تحديدَ علاقةٍ
بين رقمين غير متلاصقين.
ولكن ليس مُهِمّاً أن يحبني الله
لا أحدَ في هذا العالم ــ حتى ممّن صَلَحت أعمالُهم ــ
يستطيع أن يُقدّم دليلاً واحداً، على أن الله يحبه.

يُمكنني أن أفتحَ الباب، وأُغلقَه خلفي
بهدوء، كي لا يستيقظَ حبيبي.

SOLITUDE EXERCISES

He sleeps in the next room, a wall between us.
I am not being symbolic here,
only that there is a wall between us.
I can cover it with pictures of my lover
smoking or thinking.
But I must find a neutral place for them,
respecting the distance between us.

It seems God does not love me.
I am old enough to believe that
God has not loved me for a long time, not since
he loved the math teacher
and gave him sharp eyesight
and colored chalks
and many chances to torture a girl like me
who cannot divine the link
between two non-consecutive numbers.

But it's not important that God love me.
No one in this world, not even the righteous ones,
can prove that God loves him.

I can open the door and shut it
softly so my lover does not wake.
A girl who goes out to the street
without a place to shelter her
is not dramatic at all.

بنتٌ تنزل الشارع بدون أيّ مكان
يمكنها اللجوءُ إليه
أمرٌ ليس دراماتيكياً على الإطلاق.

عندما قال ديستويفسكي:
"لا بد للواحدِ من بيتٍ ما، يتسطيع الذهابَ إليه"
كان يتحدّث عن بشر كلاسيكيين،
لهم سوالفُ طويلة
ومعاطفُ تشبه الوِحدة.

أنا لا أحبُّ "الدراما"
ولا أجد ضرورةً لتفريغِ وردةٍ من بهجتها،
لتليقَ بميتٍ عزيز.

وإذا خرجتُ الآن من هُنا
سأُمسِكُ يدَ أوّل شخص يُقابلني
وسأجبره على مصاحبتي إلى مقهى جانبيّ،
سأقول له إن رجلاً ينامُ في غرفةٍ مجاورةٍ، بلا كوابيسَ،
لم تكن رأسُه في مستوى جسدي، فشلَ في أن يكون
صندوقَ قمامةٍ لي، ولو لمرة واحدة، وترك كلَّ شيء
يتسرّب إلى الشوارعِ العمومية.
وأنني يتيمة

When Dostoevsky said,
'One must have a home to go to,'
he was talking about classical people
who wore long sideburns
and overcoats resembling loneliness.

I do not like melodrama
and find no reason to empty a flower of its joy
to match it to a loved one who has died.

If I leave now
I will grab the hand of the first person I meet
and force him to go with me to a side street café.
I will tell him that a man sleeps in the next room
without nightmares,
that his head is not level with my body,
that he never became
a garbage pail for me, not even once (he let everything
scatter out into the street).

I will tell this stranger that I am an orphan,
and that I used to think that was enough to write
    good poems,
(which proved untrue),
and that I did not take good care of myself
to the point that a small inflammation in my sinuses
is about to become a tumor.

وكنتُ أظن أن هذا كافٍ لكتابة قصائدَ جيدة،
الأمرُ الذي ثبتَ فشلُه،
وأنني لم أعتنِ بنفسي كما يجب،
لدرجة أن التهاباً بسيطاً في جيوبي الأنفية
يوشك أن يتحول إلى سرطان، مع ذلك مازلت أكذبُ،
والمفروضُ أن يصيرَ الواحدُ ملائكياً، قبل موته بمُدّةٍ
كافية، كي لا يَتعبَ أصدقاؤه في البحث عن صفاتٍ
نبيلةٍ له
وأن موتي سيكون أسهلَ من تحريك قدمي اليُمنى إذا
تركني وحدي.

في مقهى جانبيّ،
سأحكي لرجلٍ لا أعرفه أشياءَ كثيرةً دُفعةً واحدة،
وسأضغط بأحبالي الصوتية،
على رغبته القديمة في أن يكون نافعاً،
فقد يأخذني لبيته، ويوقظ زوجتَه.
سأراقب خطوتَها نحوي، وهي تدْهسُ "الكليمَ" القذرَ
مثل لودر أهليّ، وأصطنع حياءً يُطمئنها، ويجعلها
تفرح بزوجها، وهو ينصحني أن أبدأ من جديد، بينما
أنا أعِدُه بتعلُّم العزفِ على آلة موسيقية، تُناسب صِغَرَ
حجمي، وأننا قد نتقابَل في أحدِ الأفراح العامة.

Yet I continue to lie (one of course
is supposed to be angelic for a little while
before dying to make it easier for one's friends
to find good things to say about him) aware
that if he leaves me, my death will be easier
than moving my right foot.

At a side street café
I will tell a man I don't know many things all at once,
and I will press my vocal cords
on his old wish to be useful.
Maybe he will take me to his house and wake his wife.
I will watch her step toward me as she
tramples a filthy rug like a tractor and as I feign
shyness to comfort her and make her feel satisfied
with her husband while he advises me to start over
and as I promise him to learn to play a musical instrument
    that matches my small frame
and to meet again during the national holidays.

I threatened all who loved me with my death
if I ever lose them.
Yet I do not think I will die for anyone's sake.
Surely, suicides must have trusted life more
than they should have, and must have thought
it was waiting for them somewhere else.

هدَّدتُ كُلَّ من أحبوني
بالموت إذا فقدتُهم،
ولا أعتقد أنني سأموت لأجلِ أحدٍ،
فالمنتحرون ـ بلا شك ـ
وَثِقوا في الحياة أكثرَ ممّا يجب،
فظَنوا أنها تنتظرهم في مكانٍ آخر.
وأنا لن أخرج من هُنا، قبل أن يموت أمامي،
سأضع أُذني على صدره، حيث السكوتُ أوضحُ من أن
تشككني فيه قِطّةٌ لها اظافرُ امرأةٍ محبطة، تحاول
بهستيريا قلبَ سلة المهملات، المليئةِ ببقايا نهارنا معاً،
سلةُ المهملات
التي أضعُها في أعلى السُلَّم
لأثبتَ للجيران أن لديَّ عائلةً آمنة.

سأمسك بأصابعك
وأتأمل دقّةً تليق بجرّاح، ليس بحاجةٍ لمشرطٍ طبيٍّ،
لنزعِ البُؤر الصديدية من جسدٍ يتآكل ذاتياً،
وأضعها في وعاءِ الثلج، وحيث لا رجفةَ هناك..
أخرجُ من هُنا...
مُتَّشحةً بالفَقْد وخفيفة.

I will not leave here before he dies in front of me.
I will place my ear to his chest where silence is so clear that
    even a cat,
with the claws of a disappointed woman hysterically trying
to topple the pail filled
with the remains of our evening together (which
I place at the top of the stairs
to prove to the neighbors that I have a good family)
will not make me doubt it.

I will hold your fingers
and watch with the precision
of a surgeon who does not need scalpels to remove
pustules from a deteriorating body.
I will place your fingers in an ice bowl where there are
    no tremors . . .
And I will leave here
clad in loss, and light.

You must die in front of me.
The death of loved ones is a wonderful opportunity to find
    alternatives.
On the East Delta train I often pick a suitable
lady who opens the coffers of her sympathy when I tell her
my mother died when I was six.

لا بد أن تموتَ أمامي.
موتُ أحبائنا فرصةٌ رائعةٌ لنبحَث عن بدائلَ.
في قطارات شرق الدلتا، تعوّدتُ أن أختارَ سيدةً
مُناسبة، تفتح لي خزانةَ تعاطُفها، عندما أُخبرها بموتِ
أمي وأنا في السادسة.

في الحقيقة
حدث هذا وأنا في السابعة،
ولكن "السادسة" تبدو بالنسبة لي أكبرَ تأثيراً،
فالأمهاتُ في منتصف العمر يُدمنّ الحُزنَ،
ربما لتبرير حِدادٍ سابقٍ لأوانِه.

والرتوشُ البسيطةُ أثناءَ الحَكْي،
لها سِحرٌ،
لن يفهمَه أبداً
من لم يضطروا لسرقة حنانِ الآخرين.

The truth is
it happened when I was seven,
but for me 'six' seems to have greater effect.
Middle-aged mothers are addicted to sadness
maybe to justify mourning before it begins.
These touch-ups in the telling
have a magic
that cannot be understood by those
who never needed to steal
kindness from others.

IMAN MERSAL   267
TRANS. KHALED MATTAWA, WITH THE AUTHOR

BIOGRAPHIES OF THE POETS

'Abid Ibn al-Abras (fl. 6th century), a pre-Islamic poet renowned for his descriptions of rainstorms.

Abu Nuwas (d. *circa* 815), Abbasid poet who was known for his wine poetry as well as his *mujun* ('obscene' or 'erotic') which he composed about both sexes.

Abu Shadi, Ahmad Zaki (1892–1955), Egyptian Romantic poet and member of the influential Apollo School.

Adonis ('Ali Ahmad Sa'id), a pre-eminent Syrian experimentalist poet and critic. His essays on Arabic poetry have heavily influenced scholarship on classical Arab literature.

Al-A'ma al-Tutili (d. *circa* 1130), a poet born in Tudela but raised in Seville who is renowned for his *muwashshah* poetry.

'Antara Ibn Shaddad (fl. 6th century), a poet said to have been born into slavery whose bravery in warfare and verses addressed to his beloved Abla form the subject of a popular epic.

Bennis, Mohammed (b. 1948), avant-garde Moroccan poet. He is also a prolific essayist and translator.

Darwish, Mahmoud (1941–2008), highly prolific Palestinian poet, celebrated for his moving imagery and multidimensional symbolic treatments of occupation and exile.

Hafsa Bint al-Hajj al-Rukuniyya (d. *circa* 1190), Granadan poet who composed love poems and elegies on Abu Ja'far Ibn Sa'id.

Ibn al-'Arabi (d. 1240), prolific Sufi poet and scholar.

Ibn Hamdis (d. 1132), Arabic poet born in Islamic Sicily.

Ibn Khafaja (d. 1139), Andalusian poet famous for his descriptions of nature.

Ibn Nubata al-Misri (d. 1366), a Mamluk-era poet who was born in Cairo and later moved to Damascus.

Abu Bakr Muhammad Ibn Quzman (fl. 11th–12th century), poet from Cordoba who preferred the vernacular Arabic *zajal* to the *qasida*. The poem featured in this anthology is a *muwashshaha*, that is a poem composed in classical Arabic with a final refrain in a colloquial register. The final refrain in this instance is in a local Romance dialect.

Ibn Sara (d. 1123), Andalusian poet from Santaren.

Abu al-Walid Ahmad Ibn Zaydun (d. *circa* 1070), a poet from Cordoba, known for his turbulent amorous relationship with the princess Wallada Bint al-Mustakfi.

Imru' al-Qays (d. *circa* 550), legendary pre-Islamic poet. His *Mu'allaqa* is one of the most celebrated poems in the Arabic poetic tradition.

Jayyusi, Salma Khadra (b. 1926), Palestinian poet, critic, scholar, anthologist, and founder of PROTA (Project of Translation from Arabic).

Jibran, Jibran Khalil (1883–1931), Lebanese poet with Romantic and Transcendentalist influences and prominent member of the Arab *mahjar* (exile), a term used to designate Levantine writers who made their careers in North and South America. Based in Boston and New York, Jibran published in both Arabic and English, and his English-language *The Prophet* was a bestseller.

Al-Khansa' (Tumadir Bint 'Amr, fl. early 7th century), a poet whose life spanned the pre-Islamic and early Islamic eras. She is famous for her elegies on her brothers.

Labid Ibn Rabi'a (fl. 7th century), highly renowned *mukhadram* poet (whose life spanned the pre-Islamic and Islamic eras). His *Mu'allaqa* is often considered paradigmatic for the so-called *qasida* or poly-thematic ode.

Abu al-'Ala' al-Ma'arri (d. 1058), famous Abbasid writer known for his cryptic verse infused with a skeptical mysticism, as well as his prose works such as *Risalat al-Ghufran* (The Epistle of Forgiveness).

al-Maghut, Muhammad (1934–2006), Syrian poet and playwright. He was a leading practitioner of the Arabic prose poem.

Majnun Layla (Qays Ibn Mulawwah, dates unknown), the hero of an Umayyad romance, or song-cycle who is generally regarded as a non-historical figure. He is probably the best known of the 'Udhri love poets, chaste characters who express their intense longing for their beloved before wasting away from lovesickness.

Maysun (fl. 7th century), daughter of an Arabian chief who married into the Umayyad Dynasty, wife of Mu'awiyya I and mother of Yazid I. The authenticity of the ascription of the verses in the 'Song of Maisuna' to her is often doubted.

Mersal, Iman (b. 1966), Egyptian poet. She works as Associate Professor of Arabic Literature at the University of Alberta.

Al-Mu'tamid Ibn 'Abbad (d. 1095), last of the Abbasid

rulers of Seville. He was a great patron of literature and an accomplished poet.

Qabbani, Nizar (1923–1998), Syrian poet renowned for his moving and accessible love poetry. He was perhaps the most popular Arabic poet of the 20th century.

Qasmuna Bint Isma'il (fl. 12th century), Granadan poet who is thought to be a descendant of Samuel ha-Nagid, one of the early composers of Hebrew *muwashshahat.*

Rabi'a al-'Adawiyya (d. 801), legendary mystical poet and saint.

al-Sayyab, Badr Shakir (1926–1964), Iraqi poet and critic, who, along with Nazik al-Mala'ika, created new 'free-verse' rhythms for Arabic poetry. His 'Rain Song' is one of the most celebrated Arabic poems of the 20th century.

al-Shabbi, Abu al-Qasim (1909–1934), Romantic poet of Tunisia who was extremely influential despite his tragically short career. His 'Will of Life', expressing the longing of a people to be free through nature imagery and symbolism, would became an anti-colonial anthem and has recently experienced a revival as a result of the 'Arab Spring'.

al-Shanfara (dates unknown), perhaps the most famous of the pre-Islamic brigand-poets. His *Lamiyya* ('Poem rhyming in L'), in which the poet rejects tribal values and subverts the paradigm of the heroic ode, is one of the most celebrated poems in the Arabic tradition, despite widespread acceptance of its dubious authenticity.

Tuqan, Fadwa (1917–2003), Palestinian poet and sister of the poet Ibrahim Tuqan. She is known for her elegies on her brother and for the forthright language of her amorous verse.

'Ulayya Bint al-Mahdi (d. 825), daughter of an Abbasid caliph known for her amorous verse.

'Umar Ibn Abi Rabi'a (fl. late 7th/early 8th centuries), an Umayyad poet renowned for his *ghazal*, or amorous verse.

Wallada Bint al-Mustakfi (d. *circa* 1091), daughter of an Andalusian Ummayad caliph, known for her forthright amorous and satirical verses as well as a number of romantic entanglements with other poets, especially Ibn Zaydun.

ACKNOWLEDGMENTS

Thanks are due to the following copyright holders for permission to reprint:

ABU NUWAS: 'O moon called forth by lament' (p. 203) and 'She sent her likeness stealing in dream' (p. 205) by Abu Nuwas, translated by Charles Greville Tuetey from *Classical Arabic Poetry* by Charles Greville Tuetey. Copyright © 1985 KPI Library. Reprinted with permission. ABU SHADI, AHMAD ZAKI: 'Evening Prayer' on page 20 in A. J. Arberry (translator), *Modern Arabic Poetry. An Anthology with English Verse Translations* (1967) © Cambridge University Press, reproduced with permission. ADONIS: 29 lines (approx. 286 words) from the poem 'This is my Name' by Adonis, in *Adonis, A Time Between Ashes and Roses*, translated by Shawkat M. Toorawa (Syracuse University Press, Syracuse, NY, 2004). Reprinted with permission from Syracuse University Press. AL-A'MA AL-TUTILI: 'Muwashshaha' by Al-A'ma al-Tutili, translated by James T. Monroe, taken from *Hispano-Arabic Poetry: A Student Anthology* by James T. Monroe (Gorgias Press). Reprinted with permission from James T. Monroe and Gorgias Press, LLC. BENNIS, MOHAMMED: 'Rose of Dust' translated by Anton Shammas for first publication in *Banipal Magazine* (Banipal 5, Summer 1999) in a feature on Mohammed Bennis. Translated from *Al-Makanou l-wathani* (The Pagan Place), Dar Toubqal, 1996. Copyright © Mohammed Bennis (poem) and Copyright © Anton Shammas (translation). Reprinted with permission from Mohammed Bennis, Anton Shammas, *Banipal Magazine* and Dar Toubqal Publishers. DARWISH, MAHMOUD: 'A Lesson from Kama Sutra' and 'We Were Missing a Present' from *The Butterfly's Burden*, translated by Fady Joudah. Copyright © 2007 by Mahmoud Darwish. Translation

277

TITLES IN EVERYMAN'S LIBRARY
POCKET POETS

Emily Dickinson
Letters
ED. EMILY FRAGOS

Emily Dickinson
Poems
ED. PETER WASHINGTON

John Donne
Poems and Prose
ED. PETER WASHINGTON

T. S. Eliot
Poems (US only)
ED. PETER WASHINGTON

Ralph Waldo Emerson
Poems
ED. PETER WASHINGTON

Robert Frost
Poems (US only)
ED. JOHN HOLLANDER

Thomas Hardy
Poems
ED. PETER WASHINGTON

George Herbert
Poems
ED. PETER WASHINGTON

Gerard Manley Hopkins
Poems and Prose
ED. PETER WASHINGTON

James Joyce
Poems and a Play

Langston Hughes
Poems (US only)
ED. DAVID ROESSEL

John Keats
Poems
ED. PETER WASHINGTON

Rudyard Kipling
Poems
ED. PETER WASHINGTON

Don Marquis
The Best of Archy and Mehitabel

Andrew Marvell
Poems
ED. PETER WASHINGTON

Edna St. Vincent Millay
Poems

John Milton
Poems
ED. PETER WASHINGTON

Wolfgang Amadeus
Mozart
Letters
TRANS. LADY WALLACE
ED. PETER WASHINGTON &
MICHAEL ROSE

Sylvia Plath
Poems (US only)
ED. DIANE WOOD
MIDDLEBROOK

Edgar Allan Poe
Poems and Prose
ED. PETER WASHINGTON

Alexander Pushkin
*Eugene Onegin
and Other Poems*
TRANS. CHARLES JOHNSTON

Rainer Maria Rilke
Poems
TRANS. J. B. LEISHMAN
ED. PETER WASHINGTON

Arthur Rimbaud
Poems
TRANS. PAUL SCHMIDT
ED. PETER WASHINGTON

Edwin Arlington
Robinson
Poems
ED. SCOTT DONALDSON

Christina Rossetti
Poems
ED. PETER WASHINGTON

Rumi
Poems
ED. PETER WASHINGTON

William Shakespeare
Poems
ED. GRAHAM HANDLEY

Percy Bysshe Shelley
Poems
ED. PETER WASHINGTON

Wallace Stevens
Poems (US only)

Alfred, Lord Tennyson
Poems
ED. PETER WASHINGTON

Walt Whitman
Poems
ED. PETER WASHINGTON

William Wordsworth
Poems
ED. PETER WASHINGTON

W. B. Yeats
Poems (UK only)
ED. PETER WASHINGTON

Animal Poems
ED. JOHN HOLLANDER

The Art of Angling
ED. HENRY HUGHES

*Arabic Poems:
A Bilingual Edition*
ED. MARLÉ HAMMOND

Art and Artists
ED. EMILY FRAGOS

Beat Poets
ED. KEVIN YOUNG

Blues Poems
ED. KEVIN YOUNG

Chinese Poems
TRANS. & ED.
TONY BARNSTONE &
CHOU PING

Christmas Poems (US only)
ED. JOHN HOLLANDER &
J. D. McCLATCHY

Comic Poems
ED. PETER WASHINGTON

Conversation Pieces
ED. KURT BROWN &
HAROLD SCHECHTER

The Dance
ED. EMILY FRAGOS

Doggerel (US)
Dog Poems (UK)
ED. CARMELA CIURARU

Eat, Drink and
Be Merry (US)
Poems of Food
and Drink (UK)
ED. PETER WASHINGTON

Erotic Poems
ED. PETER WASHINGTON

Fatherhood
ED. CARMELA CIURARU

The Four Seasons
ED. J. D. McCLATCHY

Friendship Poems
ED. PETER WASHINGTON

Garden Poems
ED. JOHN HOLLANDER

The Great Cat
ED. EMILY FRAGOS

Haiku
ED. PETER WASHINGTON

Indian Love Poems
ED. MEENA ALEXANDER

Irish Poems
ED. MATTHEW McGUIRE

Killer Verse: Poems of
Murder and Mayhem
ED. HAROLD SCHECHTER
AND KURT BROWN

Jazz Poems
ED. KEVIN YOUNG

Love Letters
ED. PETER WASHINGTON

Love Poems
ED. PETER WASHINGTON

Love Songs and Sonnets
ED. PETER WASHINGTON

Love Speaks Its Name:
Gay and Lesbian
Love Poems
ED. J. D. McCLATCHY

Lullabies and Poems
for Children
ED. DIANA SECKER LARSON

Marriage Poems
ED. JOHN HOLLANDER

Motherhood
ED. CARMELA CIURARU

Music's Spell
ED. EMILY FRAGOS

On Wings of Song:
Poems About Birds
(US only)
ED. J. D. McCLATCHY

Persian Poets (US)
Persian Poems (UK)
ED. PETER WASHINGTON

Poems of the American
South
ED. DAVID BIESPIEL

Poems of the American
West (US only)
ED. ROBERT MEZEY

Poems Bewitched and
Haunted
ED. JOHN HOLLANDER

Poems about Horses
ED. CARMELA CIURARU

Poems of Mourning
ED. PETER WASHINGTON

Poems of New York
ED. ELIZABETH SCHMIDT

Poems of the Sea
ED. J. D. McCLATCHY

Poems of Sleep and Dreams
ED. PETER WASHINGTON

Prayers (US)
Prayers and Meditations
(UK)
ED. PETER WASHINGTON

Railway Rhymes (UK only)
ED. PETER ASHLEY

The Roman Poets (US)
Odes, Elegies and Epigrams (UK)
ED. PETER WASHINGTON

Russian Poets
ED. PETER WASHINGTON

Scottish Poems
ED. GERARD CARRUTHERS

Solitude
ED. CARMELA CIURARU

Sonnets: From Dante to the Present
ED. JOHN HOLLANDER

Three Hundred Tang Poems
TRANS. & ED. PETER HARRIS

Villanelles
ED. ANNIE FRENCH &
MARIE-ELIZABETH MALI

War Poems
ED. JOHN HOLLANDER

Zen Poems
ED. PETER HARRIS